Secrets
of
Videoblogging

Michael Verdi
Ryanne Hodson

with Diana Weynand
and Shirley Craig

Peachpit
Press

Secrets of Videoblogging

Michael Verdi, Ryanne Hodson, Diana Weynand, and Shirley Craig

Peachpit Press
1249 Eighth Street
Berkeley, CA 94710
510/524-2178
800/283-9444
510/524-2221 (fax)
Find us on the World Wide Web at: www.peachpit.com

To report errors, please send a note to errata@peachpit.com

Peachpit Press is a division of Pearson Education

Project Editor: Deborah Branscum
Production Editor: Lupe Edgar
Tech Editor: Diane Wright
Compositor: Interactive Composition Corporation
Indexer: FireCrystal Communications
Cover design: Charlene Charles Will
Interior design: Kim Scott with Maureen Forys
Cover photos, clockwise from upper left: Annie Tsai, Charles Anthony Nealey, Stephen Garfield, GettyOne Images.
Cover photo-illustration, JoAnn Kolonick

ISBN 0-321-42917-6

9 8 7 6 5 4 3 2 1

Printed and bound in the United States of America

Dedication

*To all the videobloggers who allowed us to feature their work,
and to everyone in the vlogosphere who cheered us on and
assisted us technically—this book is dedicated
to you. Please use it to teach the world.*

Acknowledgments

A huge thanks to Nancy Ruenzel at Peachpit Press for having the foresight to publish this book; to Deborah Branscum and Marjorie Baer for correcting, clarifying and cheering; to Lupe Edgar, Scott Cowlin, Damon Hamson, Sara Jane Todd, and Gary-Paul Prince for the extra effort in making this book look good and go far; and to Diane Wright for technical editing.

From Michael and Ryanne: Big thanks to our families for putting up with our incessant videotaping and for being the stars of our videoblogs. Also, thanks for taking care of life while enduring our late night and sometimes all-day Skype calls. Much gratitude and love to Jay Dedman, Josh Kinberg, Dave Toole and Markus Sandy. Thanks to our fellow Freevloggers and master translators Pepa, Miguel, Takayuki, Richard, Fabio, Enrico, and Alessandro. And thanks to Peachpit Press for welcoming us into the family.

From Diana and Shirley: Big thanks to Tina Valinsky, who first introduced us to the world of videoblogging, and to our families who supported us while we burned the midnight oil.

Table of Contents

Chapter 7   Vlog
139

Chapter 8   Attracting an Audience
161

Epilogue
189

Exploring Videoblogs

Before you begin creating a videoblog, let's take some time to explore what other videobloggers are doing. This section will guide you to the software needed to view videoblogs, to great sites for finding other vloggers, and to specific vlogs that we particularly recommend. Videoblogs are easy to explore, but you'll need a way to keep track of all the good stuff you find, so we'll cover different ways to do that. We'll even show you how to take favorite videoblogs on the road by downloading them to mobile devices. But first, let's start by reviewing the Internet connection that's best for vloggers.

Connecting to the Internet

If you wanted to fill up your bathtub in a hurry, you'd turn the faucet on full blast. Now, if the pipe that connected the water supply to your faucet were the size of a drinking straw, turning it on full blast wouldn't be much help; you'd still get just a trickle. A dial-up Internet connection is like having a straw connecting the Internet to your computer. A broadband connection, on the other hand, is like a big fat pipe that allows for download rates that are at least 20 times faster. Most video files will start to play while they are downloading. That means you can start watching a video almost instantly—if you have broadband.

Without a high-speed connection, watching and publishing videoblogs is an exercise in frustration. Luckily, broadband is more affordable these days, especially in urban areas. So do yourself a favor and take the broadband plunge if you haven't done so already.

Updating Software and Plug-Ins

Videoblogging takes advantage of some of the latest technology. That technology, in turn, builds on features in the latest versions of the Windows XP and Mac OS X operating systems. Upgrading software is a little like building a pyramid. We'll start at the base—updating the operating systems first, then working our way up.

System Updates

To get started, your PC will need to be running Windows XP Service Pack 2. If your PC was built sometime in this millennium, odds are it has some version of XP. If you're unsure, check by going to My Computer and choosing View system information from under System Tasks (**Figure 1.1**). The window that opens up will list your system version. (Can't find it? Your PC may date from the Dark Ages. Try clicking on My Computer, then choose the About Windows item under the Help menu to get info about your elderly version of Windows.)

Figure 1.1

Windows System Properties displays your PC's current system version.

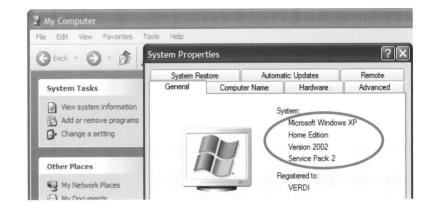

If the system information says you have something other than Windows XP installed (Windows 98 or Windows ME, for example), you'll need to upgrade to Windows XP in order to accomplish the things we'll show you in this book. If you have Windows XP Service Pack 1 installed, run the system updater to install Service Pack 2. You can automatically download and install the Service Pack 2 update by choosing Windows Update from the Start Menu (**Figure 1.2**). This will give you all of the latest security patches, the most recent version of Windows Movie Maker for editing video, and Windows Media Player for watching video.

Figure 1.2

Windows Update will automatically find and download all the updates available for your computer.

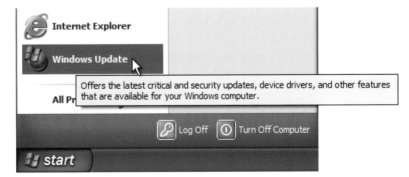

If you have a Mac, it will need OS X 10.4 or later. Any new Mac purchased in the last year should have included 10.4. You can check the version by choosing About This Mac from the Apple menu. If your Mac has 10.4, you can update to the latest version (10.4.4 at the time of this writing) by choosing Software Update from the Apple menu (**Figure 1.3**). This will give you all of the current security updates and bug fixes.

Figure 1.3
You can run Software Update anytime by selecting it through the Apple menu.

note The information in this book is written for Windows XP Service Pack 2 and Mac OS X 10.4. If your computer is using Windows XP with Service Pack 1 or Mac OS 10.3 or any older operating system, you will not be able to follow some of the instructions outlined in this book.

Web Browsers

There are a lot of Web browsers available nowadays. For videobloggers, and an increasing number of general Internet users, the browser most loved is Mozilla's Firefox (**Figure 1.4**). There are two main reasons why we recommend Firefox for videoblogging. Internet Explorer on a PC ignores the fast-start feature of QuickTime movies when they are not embedded in a Web page. So when you try to watch someone's QuickTime video (and there are a lot of those), you will probably have to wait for the entire thing to download before you can see it. Safari on a Mac has almost the same feature set as Firefox, but there is one important problem. When you use Blogger (a blog-hosting service and a big part of this book) with Safari, you lose most of the WYSIWYG (What You See Is What You Get) tools for editing your vlog, adding links, and formatting text without using HTML code.

You can certainly view other videoblogs and create your own videoblog while using Internet Explorer and Safari, but Firefox will make your life as a vlogger much easier. Give it a try. You can download the latest version of Firefox for free at www.mozilla.com.

Figure 1.4
Firefox has some cool features that Internet Explorer doesn't have yet, including tabbed browsing, integrated searching, and a popup blocker.

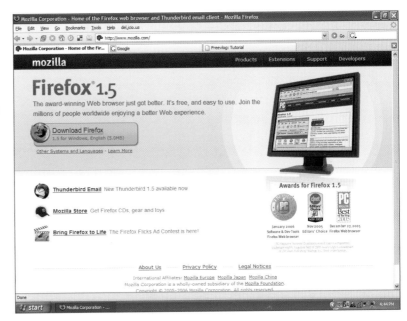

note Do you have bookmarks you don't want to lose when switching to Firefox? Firefox's Import Wizard will copy existing settings from Internet Explorer. It imports Favorites, options, cookies, stored passwords, and more. You can access the Import Wizard on installation or later by choosing File > Import.

Video Players

The three main formats for viewing videos are Windows Media, QuickTime, and Flash. Luckily, there are free Mac and PC versions of all of these players. Since you'll want to watch all kinds of videoblogs, it's important to have the most up-to-date versions.

- For PCs, download Windows Media at www.microsoft.com/windows/windowsmedia/default.mspx.

- For Macs, download Windows Media Components for QuickTime at www.microsoft.com/windows/windowsmedia/player/flip4mac.mspx.

- Download QuickTime for both PCs and Macs at www.apple.com/quicktime.

- Download Flash Player for both PCs and Macs at www.macromedia.com/go/getflashplayer.

Once downloading is complete, double-click each icon to install the new software updates.

Finding Videoblogs You'll Love

Since videoblogs are so easy and inexpensive to produce, people feel free to pursue whatever topic or audience they want, no matter how small or large. That's why vlogs cover an amazing range of genres, from the personal to the political to the comic to the educational and beyond. There's no shortage of places to find videoblogs you'll love.

Personal Picks

One way to get started is by exploring individual vlogs. Many videobloggers combine genres into an ongoing but variable showcase of their lives, while other vloggers use a more consistent, TV-show-like format. The vlogs below are some of our favorites. We can't promise that every single one will be around forever. But together they offer a great introduction to different types of videoblogs.

Geek Entertainment TV

www.geekentertainment.tv

Based in San Francisco, Geek Entertainment TV (**Figure 1.5**) covers technology and Internet-related topics with interviews of the biggest names in geekdom.

Figure 1.5
Geek Entertainment TV

29 Fragile Days

http://29fragiledays.blogspot.com

Art fans will cheer this delicate examination of the world through the eyes of a candid British lad who likes to blur the lines of reality with slow-motion camera effects and experimental sound creations (**Figure 1.6**).

Figure 1.6
29 Fragile Days

It's Jerry Time!

www.itsjerrytime.com

Jerry's mundane escapades are glorified and animated into surprisingly amusing narratives on It's Jerry Time! (**Figure 1.7**). Travel to strange and exciting places—the new bar that opened up down the street, Jerry's dingy apartment, and the city jail.

Figure 1.7

It's Jerry Time

Mom's Brag Vlog

http://nealey.blogspot.com/

Erin is a stay-at-home mother of two who uses her videoblog to document family life (**Figure 1.8**). Erin shares precious moments from first haircuts to Easter egg hunts to the birth of her second child. As a public scrapbook, Mom's Brag Vlog illustrates how a videoblog can serve as a family archive for distant relatives and future generations.

Figure 1.8

Mom's Brag Blog

Karmagrrrl

http://smashface.com/vlog/

Zadi Diaz, aka Karmagrrrl, is a Brooklyn native living in Los Angeles. Zadi's videos range from personal to political and reflect her creative and insightful character. "Tales of a karmically challenged life" is her vlog's tagline, and if it were up to us, we'd give her a big, karmic thumbs up (**Figure 1.9**).

Figure 1.9
Karmagrrl

Roger's Adventures

www.puppetkites.net

Roger's Adventures (**Figure 1.10**) come in two flavors: regular and 3D. The 3D link (on the right side of the site, under Categories) leads to videos that are like old-fashioned 3D movies but are way cooler

Figure 1.10
Roger's Adventures

because they're made by a videoblogger about his daily adventures. View them through a free pair of 3D glasses you can order at www.rainbowsymphony.com/freestuff.html.

Human Dog Laboratory

http://human-dog.com/lab

The Human Dog Laboratory offers a look into the twisted and brilliant mind of self-proclaimed professor Chris Weagel in the basement of a suburban ranch house in Michigan (**Figure 1.11**). Be afraid.

Figure 1.11
Human Dog Laboratory

Bottom Union

http://bottomunion.com/blog

Bottom Union (**Figure 1.12**) lets you see the world through the lens of an expatriate living in Holland and playing professional basketball. Creator Erik Nelson combines and transforms elements of traditional

Figure 1.12
Bottom Union

filmmaking, collage, animation, and musical composition into an engaging and dynamic dialog with his audience.

Heads Off

http://headsoff.blogspot.com

Heads Off is what you get when a graduate student in new media and a sociable programmer get together and start a videoblog. Serra and Mike (**Figure 1.13**) educate and entertain through their honest and playful video shorts.

Figure 1.13
Heads Off

Scratch Video

http://scratchvideo.tv

Scratch Video is the dark child of cinéma vérité film editor Charlene Rule. Sometimes elusive, sometimes crystalline, Charlene's videos are haunting dreams delivered through a simple whisper, a subtle gesture, a slap in the face (**Figure 1.14**).

Figure 1.14
Scratch Video

Vlog of a Faux Journalist

http://fauxpress.blogspot.com

Jan McLaughlin, the big boss at the Faux Press (**Figure 1.15**), encourages her audience and fellow vloggers with the true videoblogger's mantra: "Say what you mean; mean what you say; ask and answer any question; interview everyone."

Figure 1.15
Vlog of a Faux
Journalist

Viviendo con Fallas

http://viviendoconfallas.blogspot.com

Viviendo con Fallas, aka Life with the Fallas, is a vlog in both Spanish and English. Juan and Ximena Falla share their lives with candid and silly clips of cooking, shopping, and just dancing around the house (**Figure 1.16**).

Figure 1.16
Viviendo con Fallas

Vlog Rolls and Directories

Videobloggers usually include a "vlog roll" or list of links to their favorite vlogs (**Figure 1.17**). Some truly passionate vloggers go a step further by watching practically everything and then linking to their best discoveries. Find one vlog that you like and its vlog roll can lead to other interesting people. Examples include Josh Leo's Picks at http:// joshspicks.blogspot.com, Steve Garfield's Vlog Soup at http://steve garfield.blogs.com/videoblog/vlog_soup, and two of the authors' vlogs: The ReVlog at http://revlog.blogspot.com and Classic Videoblogs at http://freevlog.org/wordpress/index.php/category/ classic-videoblogs.

Figure 1.17

The links on vlog rolls can lead to interesting vlogs you might not find on your own. Karmagrrrl sorts her vlog roll by country.

Dedicated videoblog directories are another good way to explore videoblogs. They catalog vast numbers of vlogs and let you search for all types of videos in different ways.

Mefeedia

http://mefeedia.com

Mefeedia is a great site with a huge directory of videoblogs. (It also has many other features that we'll talk more about later.) You can click on the Directory link to search for videoblogs or browse through them alphabetically or by their popularity ranking. Or click on the Tags link (**Figure 1.18**) to search for individual videos by their tags, or keywords. Many of the vlog listings include short descriptions and reviews.

Figure 1.18

The Mefeedia directory lets you search for videoblogs by keyword, topic, and location.

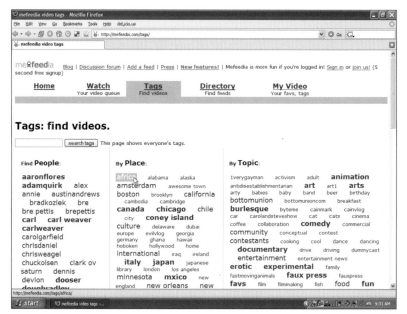

VlogDir

http://vlogdir.com

VlogDir is another terrific directory (**Figure 1.19**). It features lists of the newest and most visited videoblogs. It also has randomly featured vlogs. You can even watch a preview video from each vlogger to get a sense of what they're about.

Figure 1.19
VlogDir has a large list of vlog categories, which is another great way to find vlogs of interest.

VlogMap

www.vlogmap.org/map.php

VlogMap is a Google Map that's been hacked (it's okay, Google's cool with it) to show you the location of videobloggers all over the world (**Figure 1.20**). You can easily find videobloggers in your hometown, or others in faraway places you'd like to see. Just zoom in on an area and click on a red dot to get a link to a videoblogger's site.

Figure 1.20
VlogMap shows the global videoblogging community as tiny pins in a Google Map.

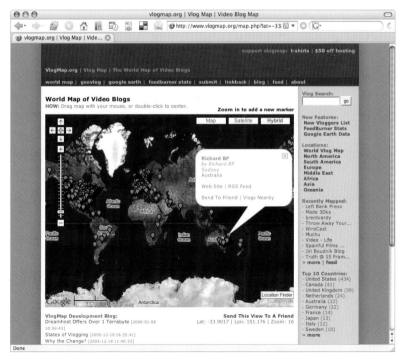

FireAnt

http://fireant.tv

FireAnt has a videoblog directory (**Figure 1.21**) that you can access from its Web site or from within the FireAnt program. One advantage of this directory is that you can preview a featured vlog just by clicking on its video image. This saves time since you can sample many vlogs at a single site. Another plus is that you can subscribe to vlogs directly from the FireAnt home page (see "Using Video Aggregators").

Figure 1.21

The FireAnt directory lets you search for videoblogs by keyword, popularity, and featured picks.

Join the Party

One of the most important elements of a videoblog is the comments section. Let people know how their videos have affected you. Did they make you laugh? Did they make you think? Maybe you found them aggravating. Give vloggers some feedback (**Figure 1.22** and **Figure 1.23**). Leaving comments lets you join the vlogging party even before you start a videoblog. That's something you can't do with TV! Comment

Figure 1.22

Most videoblog posts link to a comments section where you can read commentary on a particular video and leave your own comments as well.

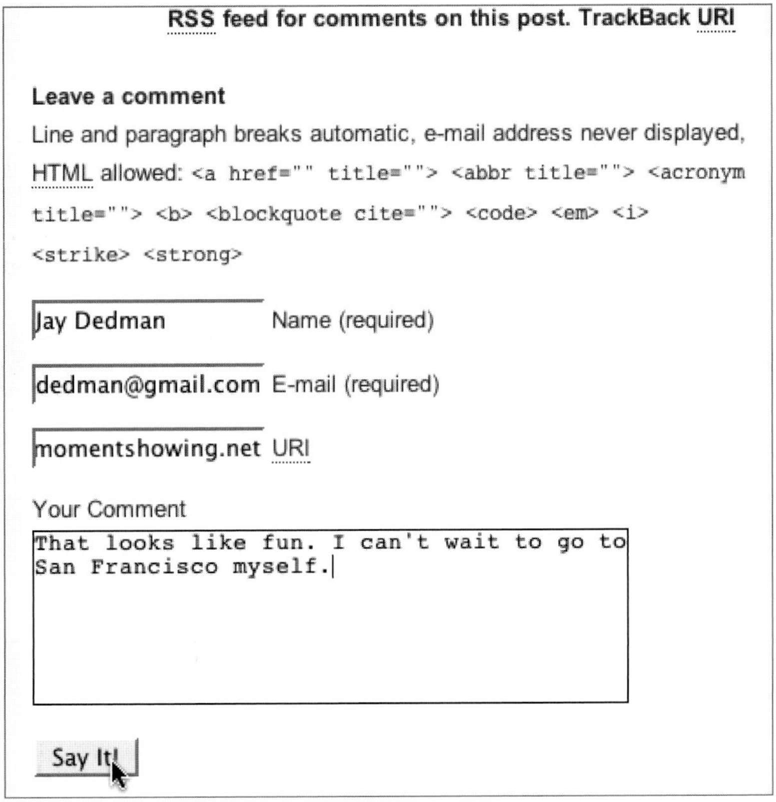

COMMUTING

COMMUTING

Here's some video from the ferry that **Ryanne** and I had to take to and from the **Macworld conference** every day.

POSTED BY VERDI ON **01.17.06** @ 10:21 AM | 8 COMMENTS | EDIT

Figure 1.23

The form for posting comments includes space for your Web site, which will be published as a link next to your comment. So every time you give feedback to other creators, you also promote your own vlog.

RSS feed for comments on this post. TrackBack URI

Leave a comment

Line and paragraph breaks automatic, e-mail address never displayed, HTML allowed: `<a href="" title=""> <abbr title=""> <acronym title=""> <b> <blockquote cite=""> <code> <em> <i> <strike> <strong>`

Jay Dedman   Name (required)

dedman@gmail.com E-mail (required)

momentshowing.net URI

Your Comment

That looks like fun. I can't wait to go to San Francisco myself.

Say It!

threads are the equivalent of community conversations and part of what makes the vlogosphere so great.

Another benefit of comments is that they include a link to the Web site of the person commenting. So checking comments is another way to find interesting videoblogs. Leaving comments on other people's vlogs is also a great way to promote your own.

Tracking Favorites

Now that you've waded through a bunch of videoblogs, found some gems, and left some comments, didn't you find it time-consuming to click on every video link on every blog? Instead of keeping track of Web sites with bookmarks, you can *subscribe* to vlogs through RSS (Really Simple Syndication) feeds and use a video aggregator to deliver them to you through the Internet. Don't worry, subscribing is free and easy. So strap on your videoblogging goggles and helmet, because you're about to embark on a subscription adventure worthy of the call to arms, "Engage!"

What Is RSS?

Technically RSS is a group of XML file formats used for Web syndication. Aren't you glad you asked? Basically, RSS is the technology that allows you to subscribe to videoblogs (and text blogs and podcasts and *The New York Times*) and have the content delivered to you automatically, rather than going to your favorite sites looking for new stuff on each page every day or every couple of hours or every fifteen minutes (yes, some of us are this obsessive). It's kind of like getting a newspaper delivered right to your door instead of walking to a newsstand to buy it. RSS allows vloggers and other publishers to send information directly to your desktop instead of forcing you to browse a page to see what's been added or updated.

RSS allows Web publishers to distribute content to anyone who wants it by creating a special file called a feed. Free Web tools let videobloggers create these feeds easily. Vloggers advertise their RSS feeds with buttons or text links that ask viewers to "Subscribe to my feed," or something similar (**Figure 1.24**). These buttons and links allow people to subscribe to the RSS feed for a particular videoblog.

Figure 1.24 RSS feed buttons, which let you subscribe to a particular videoblog, come in all shapes and sizes. The orange "signal" icon, on the far left, may become the standard now that Microsoft backs it.

The big benefit of RSS feeds is that everything is automated. Each new posting to a vlog is automatically added to the RSS feed and then sent to anyone who subscribes. That means you can easily keep track of your favorite videoblogs by subscribing to their RSS feeds with a video aggregator (see "Using Video Aggregators" below). Do that and, like magic, new videos will appear in your Web browser or on your computer's desktop. You won't have to do a thing! (Don't worry, we'll show you how to set up an RSS feed for your own videoblog in Chapter 8.)

note **Want to know more about RSS feeds? Wikipedia and Feedburner provide info at http://en.wikipedia.org/wiki/rss and www.feedburner.com/fb/a/aboutrss, respectively.**

Using Video Aggregators

If RSS is like a newspaper subscription, a video aggregator is like the paperboy who delivers it right to your door. Video aggregators are programs or Web services that you use to receive your RSS feeds. Video aggregators automatically check all of your RSS subscriptions and collect all the new content for you. There are a number of video aggregators, and new ones are sure to be developed but we recommend Mefeedia, iTunes, and FireAnt. All three are absolutely free, make it easy to subscribe to videoblogs, and work on both Macs and PCs.

Mefeedia

http://mefeedia.com

Mefeedia is a great place to find videoblogs but its main purpose is to allow you to subscribe to videoblogs and watch them directly in a Web browser. Mefeedia was built by a videoblogger for videobloggers so it has lots of great features not found anywhere else. It's easy to use and doesn't clog your hard drive with huge video files. Create a

Mefeedia user account, then follow the steps shown in **Figures 1.25** through **1.27** to check it out.

Figure 1.25
Click Mefeedia's Directory tab (or link) at the top of the page to start exploring. You can search the directory by keyword or view vlogs ranked by popularity or other qualities. After you find an interesting vlog, click on the Subscribe button to add it to your personal video queue.

Figure 1.26
Mefeedia confirms your subscription and reminds you that future videos from this vlog will be added automatically to your video queue on the Watch page.

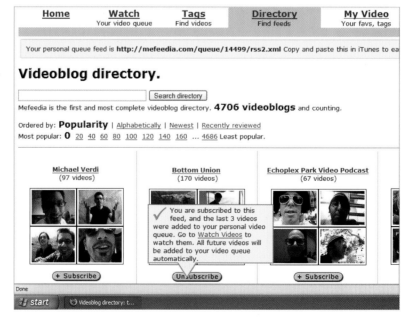

Track your subscriptions   Search by tags   Track your tags and favorites

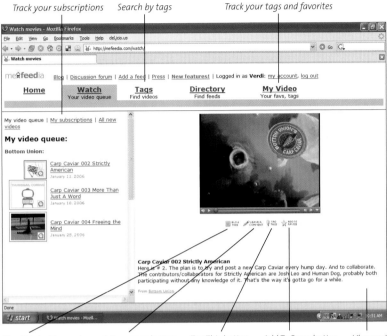

Blog This button   Leave A Comment button   Tag This button   Add To Faves button   Vlog post

Figure 1.27 To watch videos, click the Watch tab at the top of the window to go to your video queue. New videos from the vlog you've subscribed to will be listed in the left column of the Watch page. Click the title of any video to begin playing it in the right column.

Buttons below the video window let you post an item about the video on your own vlog or blog, give a vlogger feedback on the video you've seen, "tag" the video with a label or category, and add the video to your list of favorites. Mefeedia tracks the tags you create and videos you choose as favorites on the My Video page.

Mefeedia makes it easy to give vloggers feedback. Below the video window on the Watch page is a Leave A Comment button. Click the button to get a link to the comments section for the video you've just watched. If you decide to cancel your subscription to a vlog, that's easy, too. Just click on "My subscriptions" at the top of the video queue and click the Unsubscribe button.

note   **Another way to browse Mefeedia.com is to click the Tags tab to see videos in several user-created categories. Click the Queue button on a video thumbnail in any tag category to add it to your video queue for later viewing. Or watch it immediately by simply clicking the video title.**

FireAnt

http://fireant.tv

Like Mefeedia, FireAnt was created by videobloggers for videobloggers. This free desktop application allows you to subscribe, download, and watch videos in all popular formats. Unlike Web-based aggregators like Mefeedia, FireAnt will even download new videos to your Mac (**Figure 1.28**) or PC (**Figure 1.29**) automatically while you're away from the computer.

Figure 1.28

The FireAnt interface for Macs

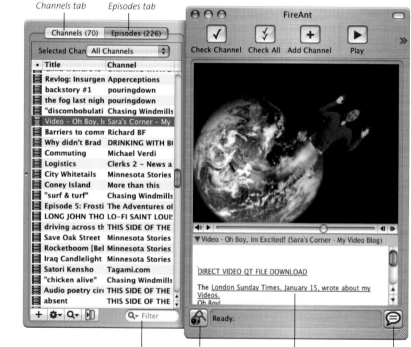

Channels tab   Episodes tab

Integrated search   Videoblog directory   Vlog post with links   Comment button

Figure 1.29

The FireAnt interface for Windows

Integrated search   Channels tab   Episodes tab   Videoblog directory   Vlog post with links

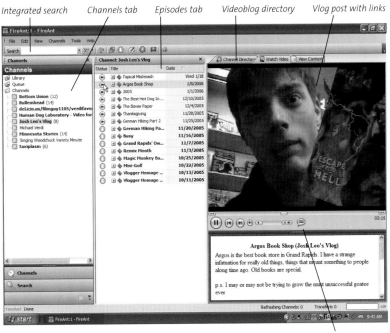

Comment button

FireAnt offers an easy way to leave comments on videos with a comment button that automatically launches your Web browser and takes you directly to the comments page for the specific video you've just viewed. FireAnt also lets you transfer videos from videoblogs to a video iPod or a Sony Playstation Player (see "Taking Vlogs on the Road").

To see how it works, download FireAnt, install it, and then open your Web browser. Find the RSS feed button on a videoblog to which you'd like to subscribe.

If you use a Mac, follow the steps in **Figures 1.30** and **1.31.**

Figure 1.30 For Macs only: Copy a vlog's RSS feed button link by pressing Control-click and choosing Copy Link Location. Open FireAnt. Click the Add Channel (+) button to subscribe to the vlog feed by adding it to your list of channels.

Figure 1.31 A window will pop up with the copied feed address automatically entered. In the Download drop-down menu, choose how many videos from the feed you want to download to your computer: Nothing, The most recent item, The last three items, or All available items. Now click the Add Channel button, and FireAnt will start downloading the videos.

If you're on a PC, follow the steps in **Figures 1.32** through **1.34**.

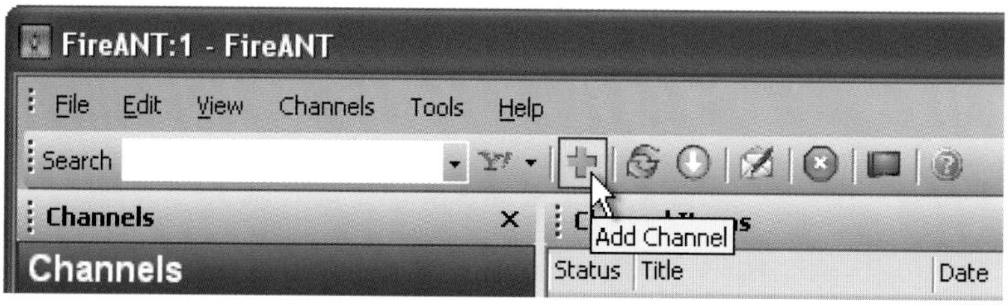

Figure 1.32 For PCs only: Copy the feed button's link by right-clicking and choosing Copy Link Location. Open FireAnt. Click the Add Channel (+) button to subscribe to the vlog feed by adding it to your list of channels.

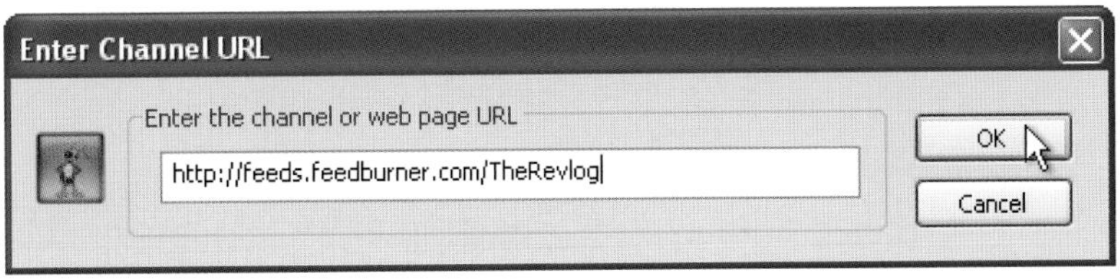

Enter Channel URL   ✕

Enter the channel or web page URL

http://feeds.feedburner.com/TheRevlog| OK

                                                        Cancel

Figure 1.33 A window will pop up. Paste the feed address that you copied in the window, then click OK.

Channel: ✕

Status | Title | Date ▽

        ⊞ ◈ Magic Magic Ma...   Mon 3:4...

Click to download r Senior-M...   Mon 9:3...

        ⊞ ◈ Sleater Kinney ...   Mon 9:2...

        ⊞ ◈ OK Go-Backyard...   Mon 9:1...

Figure 1.34 All available videos for the vlog you've subscribed to will show up in the center Channel pane of the FireAnt window. Click an orange arrow button to download a video you want to watch. (A word of caution: If you try to download many videos at once, you won't able to view anything until at least one has finished downloading.)

note FireAnt can quickly fill up your computer with gigabytes and gigabytes of video files. On a Mac, under the FireAnt menu, you can set the preferences of this program to automatically delete videos after they have been played and free up space for more videos. On a PC, you must delete old videos manually by choosing Tools > Cleanup.

iTunes

www.apple.com/itunes

It's not just for music anymore. Now you can subscribe to videoblogs and watch videos in the newest version of iTunes (**Figure 1.35**). If you don't already have it, download iTunes for the PC or Mac, then follow the steps in **Figures 1.36** through **1.39** to subscribe to a videoblog.

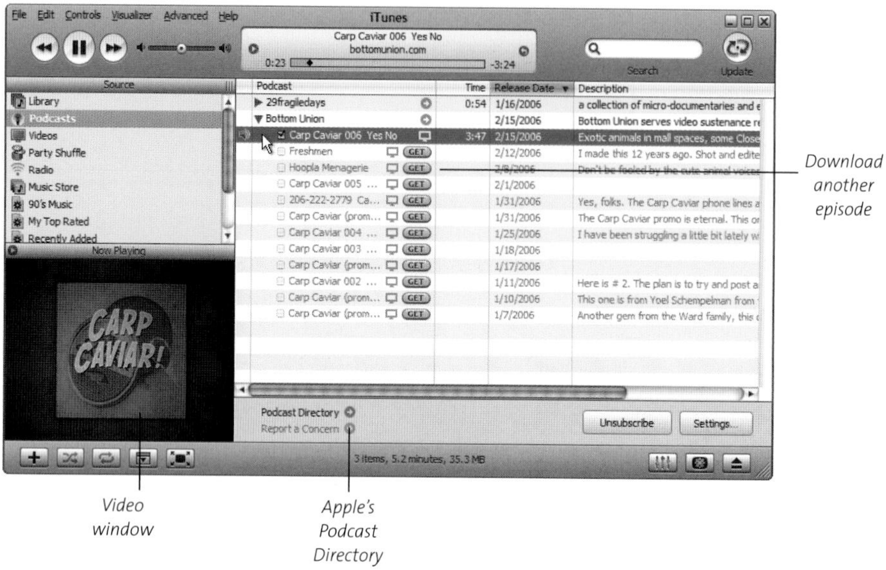

Figure 1.35   iTunes: The secret video aggregator

Figure 1.36
Go to a videoblog you'd like to subscribe to and copy its feed button link by right-clicking it (PCs) or Control-clicking (Macs) and choosing Copy Link Location. Then open iTunes and choose Advanced > Subscribe to Podcast.

Figure 1.37

Paste the copied feed link into the Subscribe to Podcast window that pops up and click OK.

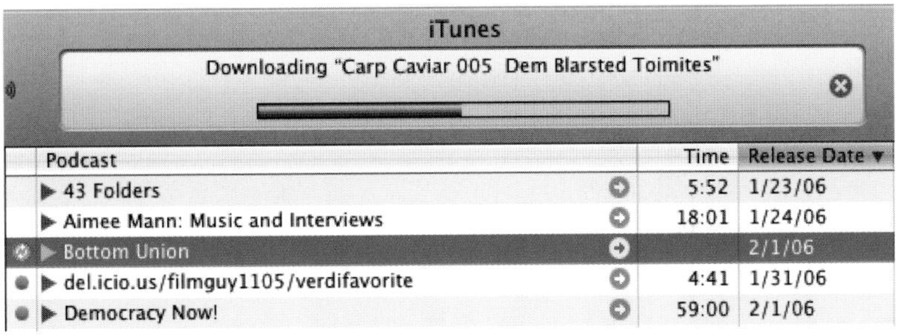

Subscribe to Podcast

URL:

feed://feeds.feedburner.com/BottomUnion

Cancel   OK

Figure 1.38

iTunes will automatically begin downloading the most recent video posted to that vlog. Once the video is downloaded, you can double-click on the title to select and view it. Or you can select it with a single click and then press the Play button to watch.

iTunes

Downloading "Carp Caviar 005 Dem Blarsted Toimites"

Podcast		Time	Release Date ▼
▶ 43 Folders	➔	5:52	1/23/06
▶ Aimee Mann: Music and Interviews	➔	18:01	1/24/06
▶ Bottom Union	➔		2/1/06
▶ del.icio.us/filmguy1105/verdifavorite	➔	4:41	1/31/06
▶ Democracy Now!	➔	59:00	2/1/06

Figure 1.39

If you want to download other videos, click the triangle next to the Podcast listing and click the Get buttons for the additional videos.

iTunes

Podcast		Time	Release Date ▼
▶ 43 Folders	➔	5:52	1/23/06
▶ Aimee Mann: Music and Interviews	➔	18:01	1/24/06
▼ Bottom Union	➔		2/1/06
☑ Carp Caviar 005 Dem Blarsted Toimites		4:42	2/1/06
☐ 206-222-2779 Carp Caviar Hotline	GET		1/31/06
☐ Carp Caviar (promo 50) StoneFace	GET		1/31/06
☐ Carp Caviar 004 Freeing the Mind	GET		1/25/06

note Both PC and Mac users can also subscribe to vlogs in iTunes by dragging and dropping feed buttons from a browser page directly into the iTunes Podcast window.

Single-Click Subscriptions

Some vlogs offer one-click subscribe buttons that do exactly what their name implies (**Figure 1.40**). They let fans of iTunes and other aggregators subscribe to vlogs with a single mouse click.

Figure 1.40

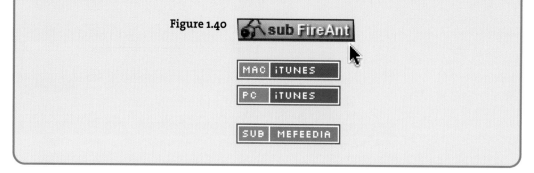

You can also subscribe to vlogs, which Apple calls *video podcasts*, in the built-in Podcast Directory. The biggest downside to iTunes is that it plays QuickTime movies only. Many videobloggers use Windows Media or Flash Video, and you won't be able to view their videos with iTunes. Another disadvantage is that iTunes does not link back to videoblogs for commenting.

Taking Vlogs on the Road

If you've subscribed to vlogs using video aggregators, you can now take your favorite ones with you. Apple's new iPod and Sony's PlayStation Portable (PSP) make it possible to watch video on the go. There is a catch—each device is pretty picky about what kind of video it will play.

- The Apple iPod plays only certain QuickTime videos. Thankfully, vloggers will usually let you know if their stuff is compatible with the iPod.

- The Sony PSP will play only a specially formatted .mp4 file. Most videoblogs don't offer videos in this format. That means you'll have to convert the videos yourself—unless you use FireAnt on a PC, which can convert the videos for you automatically.

- Internet-enabled mobile phones will play anything labeled 3GP.

iPod with Mefeedia

Mefeedia also offers a way to get videos onto your iPod. When you create an account at Mefeedia, the site creates a master feed of all the videoblogs you've subscribed to in your video queue page. Subscribe to this feed in iTunes, and it will automatically download new videos and put them on your iPod when you sync it. Here's how:

1. Log in to Mefeedia. Simply copy your personal queue feed at the top of the Home page (**Figure 1.41**).

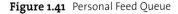

Figure 1.41   Personal Feed Queue

2. In iTunes, choose Advanced > Subscribe to Podcast. Paste the feed address into the pop-up window and click OK (**Figure 1.42**).

Figure 1.42
Subscribe to Podcast

iPod with FireAnt

If you own a Mac and use FireAnt as your aggregator, you can simply select the videos in FireAnt you'd like to put on your iPod, choose the gear-shaped icon in the lower left corner of the FireAnt window, and choose Send to iTunes (**Figure 1.43**).

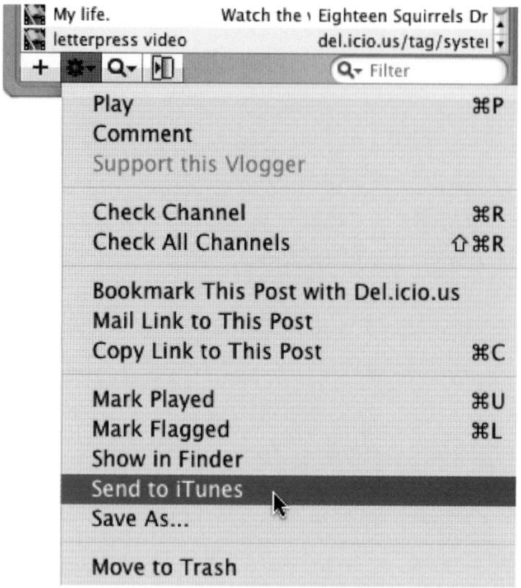

Figure 1.43

On a Mac, FireAnt can send your videos to iTunes for automatic iPod syncing.

It's also easy to transfer videos to your iPod on a Windows PC. Simply follow the steps in **Figures 1.44** and **1.45**.

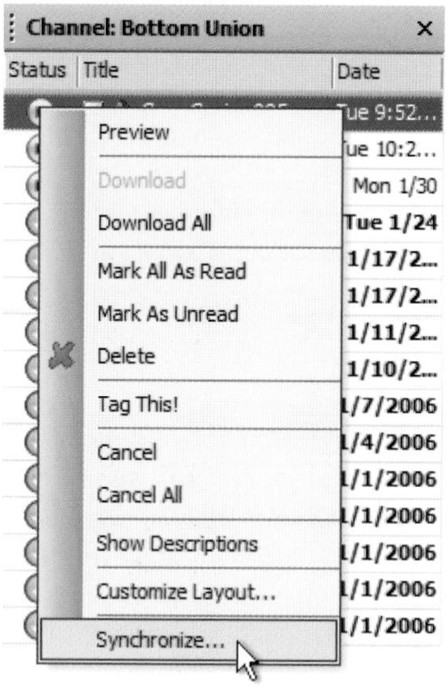

Figure 1.44

Open FireAnt and select the videos that you'd like to put on your iPod. Now right-click on them and choose Synchronize.

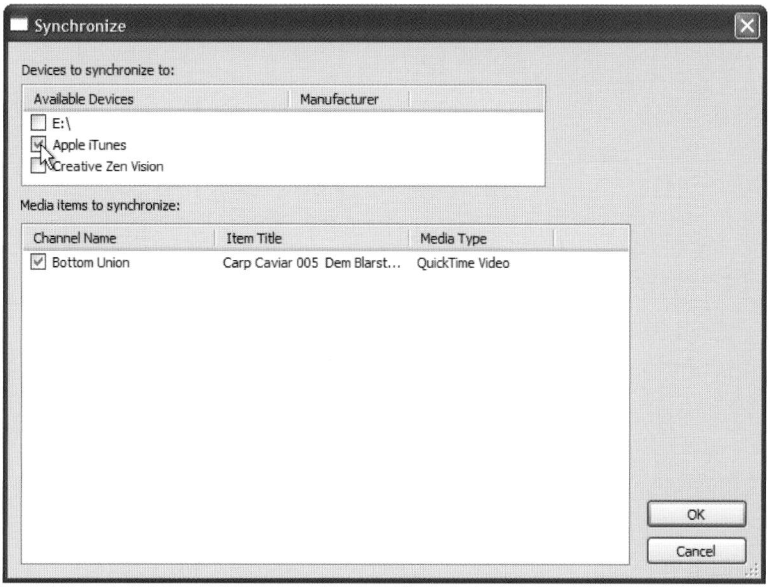

Figure 1.45

In the dialog that pops up, select Synchronize > Apple iTunes and then click OK.

These steps will send iPod-compatible videos to iTunes for automatic iPod syncing. The next time you sync your iPod, you will see a FireAnt playlist with videos from your favorite videoblogs.

iPod with iTunes

Transferring your videos to the iPod is super easy using iTunes. Simply connect the iPod to your computer. iTunes will automatically transfer all compatible videos from your vlog subscriptions to your iPod.

note iPods that play video support certain QuickTime videos only. If the format of your favorite videoblog isn't supported, iTunes won't transfer it to your iPod. Developers at Mefeedia and FireAnt are working on the ability to convert all formats for syncing and playing on the iPod.

PSP with FireAnt (PC Only)

Sony's PSP is another great device for watching videoblogs on the run. With FireAnt as your aggregator, you can easily download videoblogs from your PC to a PSP.

1. Open FireAnt and choose View > Media Items. Right-click on a video in the Media Inbox that you want to put on your PSP.

2. Choose Synchronize > Sony PSP (**Figure 1.46**).

Figure 1.46
FireAnt lets you download your favorite videoblogs to a PSP.

3. In the PSP Synchronization Settings box, click Sync (**Figure 1.47**). FireAnt will begin preparing the video for PSP syncing.

Figure 1.47
FireAnt's PSP Synchronization Settings

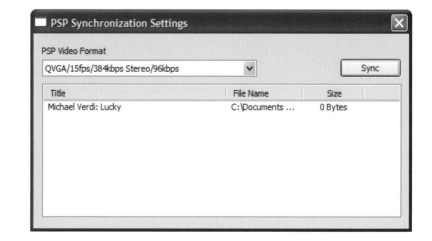

4. Plug the PSP into your computer using a USB cable.

5. Turn on the PSP.

6. On your PSP, choose Settings > USB Mode. Videos will automatically sync to your PSP in the Video Category.

Mobile Phones

Many new mobile phones can browse the Internet and play videos in the 3GP format. While mobile phones have the potential to become a popular video playback device, as of this writing only a few videobloggers make videos in 3GP format. Because video aggregators don't yet support mobile phone technology, the only way to download 3GP video is by going directly to vlogs that support it.

Rocketboom, a daily news satire, and MobuzzTV are two sites that specialize in mobile video, are two sites that support the 3GP mobile phone format. Though you can't subscribe to a feed, you can view 3GP videos from 3G phones at http://rboom.com and http://mobile.mobuzz.com.

2

Finding Your Story

Vlogging may not get you your 15 minutes of fame but it will probably make you famous to at least 15 people. What counts is that you are making content that is true to your ideas and passions. So in this chapter we'll explore vlogging styles in more depth. We'll help you pick a topic, set the tone, and find an audience for your videoblog. Finally, we'll offer guidelines for videoblogging within ethical and legal bounds.

Exploring Different Styles

In Chapter 1, we briefly explored some of the different vlog genres or styles. Not all videobloggers use a specific or consistent format, and one is certainly not required. To give you some ideas for the style of your own videoblog, let's take a look at additional vlogs in more detail. As you explore, pay attention to the styles or formats that you find most appealing. Try to think of a story you want to tell and how you might use your voice to tell it. The most engaging videoblogs reflect the personality of the vloggers behind them.

Vlogs as Personal Journals

A vlogger's own life is by far the most popular vlog subject and format. Autobiographical videoblogs may jump from topic to topic with individual entries but tend to stick to a few main themes overall. The authors' personal vlogs are good examples. They usually feature stories about friends and family, videoblogging itself, art, collaboration, and music.

Ryanne's "En Route" video, at http://ryanedit.blogspot.com/2005/11/en-route.html, combines several of these elements (**Figure 2.1**). A friend in the Netherlands asked her to send the packaging from a certain brand of butter for an art project. Instead of simply emailing the friend to say she'd sent the butter, Ryanne made a video showing herself walking to a grocery store, buying a package of butter, and then shipping the package overseas. This video was a collaborative project with fellow videoblogger Erik Nelson of www.bottomunion.com/blog.

Figure 2.1
With "En Route," Ryanne turned a seemingly mundane task into a collaborative music video.

Like personal journals, personal videoblogs can serve as a kind of scrapbook or archive of your life. After a few years of vlogging, you can look back into the archives for an insight into what was happening in your life at that time, what was different then compared to now, and what you found important during that period. Documenting the people in your life can also create an invaluable and precious record for generations to come. Videoblogging is also a modern way to preserve oral history and generational storytelling.

Michael's video "Wishbone," at http://michaelverdi.com/index.php/2005/11/27/wishbone, is one illustration of the value of personal vlogging (**Figure 2.2**). When Michael asks his father about how he feels, nine days after open heart surgery, his dad responds with an unexpected riff on wishbones, winning, and losing. The image of Michael's father delivering his philosophy while inadvertently displaying the massive surgical scar down his chest creates a powerful impact and preserves a moment in time that will surely be cherished by his great-great grandchildren.

Figure 2.2
In "Wishbone," Michael documents a personal moment with his father that will be archived for posterity.

Vlog Shows

Some videobloggers create vlog "shows" by focusing on a particular topic that they present in a similar way each time. Shows can be about any subject matter, including politics, art, comedy, science, and music. Bill Streeter's Lo-Fi St. Louis is a great example. Bill covers the local

St. Louis music scene at http://lofistl.com. Most of his videos consist of a short introduction followed by footage of a band playing live in a bar (**Figure 2.3**).

Figure 2.3

Fans of live, independent music will love Lo-Fi St. Louis.

Steve Garfield produces "The Carol and Steve Show" and stars in it with his wife, Carol. This "real" reality TV show includes homey videos of the married couple shoveling snow, enjoying a ballgame at Boston's Fenway Park, and sitting and chatting in their kitchen (**Figure 2.4**). View it at http://stevegarfield.blogs.com/videoblog/carol_and_steve_show.

Chasing Windmills is the fictional story of a young couple that's written and acted by another engaging real-life pair, Cristina Cordova and Juan Antonio (**Figure 2.5**). View it at http://chasingmills.blogspot.com.

Figure 2.4   Become virtual neighbors and explore Boston with Carol and Steve, a "real" reality TV couple.

Figure 2.5 In "Ay Consuela," Cristina and Juan argue over hiring an immigrant worker to clean their apartment.

Experimental Vlogs

Adam Quirk and Brian Gonzalez are two vloggers who like to experiment and bring their audience along for the ride. Adam mixes animation, computer-generated speech, still images, and video in imaginative ways. The Singing Woodchuck Variety Minute can be found at http://bullemhead.com/ woodchuck (**Figure 2.6**). Brian is a film student whose video "Precipice," at http://gnitseretni .blogspot.com/2005/09/ precipice.html, has become an instant classic (**Figure 2.7**). The beautifully edited black-and-white images grab your attention and keep it until the end, when the video unexpectedly blossoms into full color.

Figure 2.6   The wacky Singing Woodchuck Variety Minute always leaves you wanting more—more witty, animated rodents, that is.

Figure 2.7   Brian Gonzalez's classic, "Precipice," tells a compelling story in an unexpected way.

Citizen Journalism

Citizen journalism allows people to redefine what is newsworthy and participate in a form of communication traditionally closed to nonprofessionals. In the case of videoblogging, these are videos made by everyday people about events and issues that may not be covered by mainstream media outlets. Most citizen journalists don't act like TV reporters and shoot themselves live at the scene of an incident like we see on the 11 o'clock news. It's more common that news stories covered by vlogging citizen journalists highlight what people in a given community care to about, and so they vary depending on what is important to particular vloggers and their community.

Figure 2.8
The Bad Waitress, a restaurant in South Minneapolis, gets a good review from local diners on Minnesota Stories, www.mnstories.com.

Take Minnesota Stories, for example. This daily videoblog by state residents is an evolving showcase for local citizen media. It spotlights personal stories and commentaries on local politics, independent films, music, and eateries, the kind of little gems that fall through the cracks of mainstream media (**Figure 2.8**).

A journalistic approach doesn't work for every video or every topic, but sometimes it's exactly what you want. New Yorker Jonny Goldstein, for example, got impatient when the Columbia Branch Library in his low-income neighborhood was closed for more than a year. When renovation work ground to a halt, he used his vlog to push for change (**Figure 2.9**). View his video at www.jonnygoldstein.com/ 2005/08/21/reopen_ the_library.php.

Figure 2.9
Citizen journalists often tackle local issues. Jonny Goldstein asks for help from New York City politicians in "Reopen the Library."

Topic, Tone, and Audience

The huge variety of videoblogs is part of what makes the vlogoshere so endlessly fascinating. People enjoy all kinds of vlogs. Your mission, first and foremost, is to create a videoblog that showcases your passions. The magic of the Internet and videoblogs is that your audience will eventually find you.

Choosing a Topic

The standard advice to beginning writers is to write about what you know. That's a good suggestion for videobloggers, too, and helps explain why personal videoblogs are so popular. After all, we're all experts about our own lives. Does the idea of sharing your life sound like fun? If you'd love to show the highlights (or lowlights) of a vacation or produce a clip of your pet's antics in the park, an autobiographical vlog may be right for you. Think about shooting a day in your own life as the first video for your vlog.

If a day-in-the-life approach is not appealing, ask yourself a few questions. What are you an expert on or what are you passionate about? Perhaps you collect Japanese Manga comics or a specific kind of pottery. Maybe you're a novice gardener who loves orchids and wants to use a vlog to record your progress with them. You can build a videoblog around virtually any personal interest or skill. What's the story you want to tell? Think of a topic right now you'd like to share in your first vlog.

Setting the Tone

Once you decide on a topic, it's time to think about approach and tone. Your tone will depend on whichever part of your personality you choose to show in your video. Are you exhibiting the professional, expert side in an educational video? Are you being sarcastic in a political commentary video? Are you feeling poetic, comic, mysterious? Many vloggers choose to mix up the tone on their videoblogs by switching from one approach to another, reflecting how varied they are as people. Many switch from serious to artistic, depending on their mood and the idea behind a video. One video might be a scathing editorial on current events, the next could be a funny moment recorded at random. Your tone is a reflection of your personality, just as the vlog you create is an extension of who you are.

Knowing Your Audience

Another critical part of creating a vlog is figuring out who you're speaking to and how to reach them. Is it just your family and friends?

Or is it a specific target group such as twenty-somethings, political junkies, musicians, or marketers? Thinking about your intended audience will help you set the tone of your vlog. You don't want to make many in-jokes if you hope to reach a large number of people who don't already know you and understand the jokes. But if your target audience is just your college buddies, then you can be as much of an insider as you'd like.

Vlogging is a public act, and yet one of the wonders of vlogging is that no matter how carefully you target a particular audience in creating and posting video, that audience may fail to show up. On the other hand, an entirely unexpected group may drop by to enjoy the show. In short, you can never predict exactly who will love your videos. Birdwatcher Alan Larson, for example, created a vlog for bird watchers that uses terms tailored to that audience (**Figure 2.10**). But Alan's BirdCam Blog, is so beautiful and unusual that it has attracted a much broader audience than Alan originally imagined, ranging from artists to professional videographers to little kids .

Figure 2.10

A video of affectionate cardinals feeding each other seeds is one of the pleasures of Alan's BirdCam Blog http://birdcamblog .blogspot.com.

You will never know from day to day exactly who is watching your videoblog. You might educate a few people on a favorite topic or draw an audience of hundreds, even thousands. Fuel your videoblog with enthusiasm and, eventually, your audience will find you.

Capturing People and Places

The idea of videotaping anyone you want, anywhere you want, and then publishing the results on your vlog may seem appealing. But in most cases you need permission from the people you tape in order to publish your footage on the Internet. You also need permission to use any copyrighted material in your vlog, including any of the commercial

CDs and DVDs in your collection, and things you see on TV. So in this section we'll give you some broad guidelines for vlogging within legal and ethical bounds.

> **note** **Keep in mind that we are not attorneys. What follows is general information about legal issues, not legal advice. Follow these guidelines at your own risk, and please consult an attorney about any questions or concerns you have about legal rights and responsibilities related to videoblogging.**

Taping in Public

Sometimes people get really uncomfortable when they're being videotaped. If you've ever flashed a camcorder around a family event, it's more than likely that at least one person has tried to hide from the camera lens and said, "Please, don't tape me." Imagine how invasive it must feel to those folks to see a stranger taping them without permission. For both ethical and legal reasons, we recommend three rules for happy vlogging:

- Always ask for permission before you start videotaping.

- Document, in one form or another, that you've received permission to tape—and keep those permissions on file.

- Always respect other people's wishes.

The same rules apply even if you are shooting in a public place, such as a park, airport, or subway station. Even though people who are sitting on a park bench or walking down the street are fully aware that they're in public, it's rude to stick your video camera in someone's face unless you've asked permission first. What if you're shooting a crowd scene? Here's a good rule of thumb: **If an individual you want to videotape will be recognizable in any footage you shoot for your vlog, then you need that person's permission to proceed.**

Even after you get permission to videotape, it's a good idea to be obvious about the fact that you are shooting video so no one thinks you're trying to shoot without permission. If you're shooting on private property, such as at a mall or in a grocery store, don't be surprised if you're asked to stop. Many property owners prohibit videotaping on their premises.

Getting Permission to Shoot

An easy way to get an authorized permission is to simply ask subjects before you begin shooting if it's okay to videotape them for your videoblog. If they say yes, tell them you would like to record their consent. Point your camera at the subject, begin recording, then repeat the question: "Is it okay if I videotape our conversation in this location for use in my videoblog on my Web site?"

If your subject is not a friend or family member, ask them to say and spell out their full name and contact information on the tape. We like to ask for that info so we can send our subjects a link to the video masterpieces they've participated in. People are usually happy to share the info. If they're not, you can reassure worrywarts that their contact information will stay confidential and will be not be included in the final video on your Web site. That means, of course, that you must keep your promise and never, ever, release their contact info on your vlog or anywhere else without their permission.

Another way of getting approval is by having your subject sign a permission form, also called a release form, such as the one pictured in **Figure 2.11**.

Whether your permission forms are on paper or on video, make sure you keep all of them on file and easy to locate. If a neighbor decides he looks awful instead of adorable on your vlog, for example, he may forget that he ever agreed to be videotaped. Permission forms are a type of protection, so don't lose them.

Videotaping Children

Anyone under the age of 18 is a minor. Before you videotape children or teenagers, you must get the consent of their parents or guardians. Remember your manners and ask the children or teenagers for permission as well.

Videotaping and Videoblogging Permission Form

I, _____ , (*subject's name*) agree to allow _____ (*videoblogger's name*) to videotape me and consent to the use of my likeness on such videotape without compensation.

I agree to allow these video images to be used at the sole discretion of (*videoblogger's name*) on the videoblog located at (*videoblog URL here*) and throughout the World Wide Web and in perpetuity.

I understand that these images will be archived and will be accessible to any person visiting (*videoblog URL here*) for as long as the videoblog exists.

Subject's signature

X _____

Parent's signature (if subject is a minor)

X _____

Date: _____

Contact Information:
Subject's name   _____
Subject's email   _____
Subject's phone   _____

Figure 2.11 You need a release to show people's liknesses in your vlog.

Using Others' Materials

It would be great to spice up your videos by grabbing a song from one of your favorite bands or a clip from your favorite film. Fight that impulse! There are pretty stiff regulations written to prevent you, and everybody else, from recycling stuff illegally. Generally speaking, it's either impossible or prohibitively expensive for an individual to get permission to use material from songs, music, movies, or photos copyrighted under U.S. law and registered with the U.S. Copyright Office.

There are some exceptions, most notably the "fair use" provision of copyright law, which allows people to quote from or use part of a copyrighted work under certain conditions. The Stanford University's online Copyright and Fair Use Center describes it this way:

> "Fair use is a copyright principle based on the belief that the public is entitled to freely use portions of copyrighted materials for purposes of commentary and criticism. For example, if you wish to criticize a novelist, you should have the freedom to quote a portion of the novelist's work without asking permission. Absent this freedom, copyright owners could stifle any negative comments about their work. Unfortunately, if the copyright owner disagrees with your fair use interpretation, the dispute will have to be resolved by courts or arbitration. If it's not a fair use, then you are infringing upon the rights of the copyright owner and may be liable for damages."

Using copyrighted material for business reasons is not considered fair use, so you can forget about using "Born to Be Wild" as the soundtrack for a video on your uncle's car dealership vlog. But even non-commercial use can be tricky. The U.S. Copyright Office explains the problem this way: "The distinction between 'fair use' and infringement may be unclear and not easily defined. There is no specific number of words, lines, or notes that may safely be taken without permission. Acknowledging the source of the copyrighted material does not substitute for obtaining permission." When in doubt, leave it out or seek legal advice.

Copyrights and Copy Wrongs

You can learn more about copyright law at the US Copyright Office's Web site at www.copyright.gov. Stanford University's online Copyright and Fair Use Center, at http://fairuse.stanford.edu, includes a "Copyright & Fair Use Guide" that's packed with helpful resources.

Creative Commons Licenses

The legal headaches involved in using copyrighted material are one reason why videobloggers often love to remix and use each other's material. A nonprofit organization called Creative Commons has made that simple to do by developing flexible and voluntary "some rights reserved" copyright licenses for creative works (**Figure 2.12**). Creative Commons licenses spell out exactly how an individual's audio, video, images, or text may be used by others. That's why the use of Creative Commons licenses is encouraged by many in the videoblogging and blogging communities.

Figure 2.12

Creative Commons offers flexible, customizable ways to license your videos and share them with others (http://creativecommons.org).

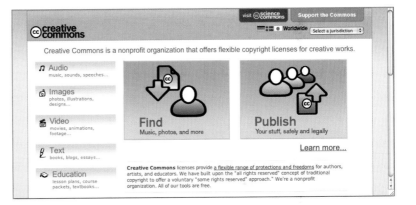

Licensing Through Creative Commons

A Creative Commons license is an easy way for vloggers to protect their videos while sharing them with the world. Simply go to http://creativecommons.org/license and fill out a short form to select the license you want. (If you need guidance, the site has plenty of info and tutorials to help you make a decision.) After you've made a selection, the site will automatically create the HTML code for a Creative Commons button (**Figure 2.13**) and explain how to add the code to your vlog.

Figure 2.13

Why a button? "The button is designed to act as a notice to people who come in contact with your work that your work is licensed under the applicable Creative Commons license," the site explains. The HTML code also includes "metadata that enables Creative Commons-enabled search engines," to locate your work so that other people can find out about it.

Creative Commons offers six main licenses. As explained at http://creativecommons.org/about/licenses/meet-the-licenses, the most restrictive license is Attribution Non-commercial No Derivatives, abbreviated as "by-nc-nd" (**Figure 2.14**). This license is known as the "free advertising" license because it allows people to download your works and share them with others as long as they give you credit and link back to your Web site. But under the terms of the license, they are not allowed to change the works in any way or use them commercially.

Figure 2.14 Creative Commons uses abbreviations and symbols to indicate the terms of a license. The "by-nc-nd" (non-commercial/no derivatives) license is the most restrictive.

The least restrictive license is called Attribution (by), which allows people to do virtually anything with your work, including use it commercially, as long as they give you credit for the original. Attribution Non-commercial Share Alike, abbreviated as "by-nc-sa" is the license most commonly used by videobloggers (**Figure 2.15**). That's because it offers the greatest flexibility for people to "remix, tweak, and build upon your work as long as they do it non-commercially." With this license, people who use your work must credit you, and any creations based on your original must be licensed under the same terms.

Figure 2.15 Most vloggers who license their work under a Creative Commons license choose Non-commercial Share Alike, abbreviated as "by-nc-sa," because it gives them credit for their work while still allowing others to remix their video gems.

Check out the Creative Commons Web site to learn more about the rights, restrictions, and full legal code for each license. Licensing your work through Creative Commons is a terrific way to protect and promote your videoblog. As we discuss in the next chapter, it's also a great source of cool stuff to play with on your own vlog.

Checking Your Toolbox

Now that you've gotten a feel for other videoblogs, it's time to make sure you have all the essential tools for creating your own videos and uploading them to the Web. Besides a computer and an Internet connection, you'll need a camera to shoot your masterpiece and video-editing software to edit the sure-to-be-fabulous footage. You may also want to consider using audio-editing applications that improve your video's sound. Let's look inside the videoblogger's toolbox we recommend.

Picking a Camera

Cameras come in all shapes and sizes. There are DV cameras, HDV cameras, DVD cameras, and digital still cameras that shoot video. You can edit and prepare clips for the Web using video from almost any camera, but not all cameras make it easy.

If you're still using an old VHS cinder block, for example, it's time to upgrade. That's because VHS is an analog format, and video-editing software uses digital format. You can buy a converter box to get VHS footage onto your computer, but that will cost about as much as a new camera. The same goes for old 8mm and Hi-8 cameras (see "Moving from Analog to Digital").

note **If you plan to include old video footage—something from that birthday party in 1972, perhaps—you'll just have to bite the bullet and convert it. There are commercial services that can do it for you, so you don't have to spring for your own converter box**

DVD camcorders that record directly to DVD are growing in popularity. These are great for playing what you shot back on your television. However, they can be a pain for vlogging if you want to edit this footage on your computer. The files created by DVD camcorders are incompatible with many video-editing programs, which means that the DVD video has to be converted into an editing-friendly format. Buying conversion software isn't wildly expensive ($100 or less) but using it may be time consuming. Again, you might want to use a commercial service for this.

If you plan to buy a new camera, keep in mind that the latest and greatest gadgets are not necessarily the best for videoblogging. Here's why: Video images are composed of "picture elements," or pixels. For each video format a specific number of pixels make up each horizontal line of an image, and a specific number of pixel lines run from the top to the bottom of the image. A high-definition camera, for example, can capture an image that is 1920 pixels across and 1080 lines of pixels top to bottom (referred to as 1920 by 1080). That totals a whopping 2,073,600 pixels worth of visual information *per frame*.

The quality of a video image is influenced by the number of pixels it contains. Usually more pixels mean higher quality because more information is captured about an image's color, luminosity, and movement. Video shot by a high-definition camera will look gorgeous playing on an HD screen, but that's not where your vlog will be playing. When you prepare video for the Web, you'll need to shrink the original video down to a frame size of 320 by 240 pixels, essentially throwing away 96 percent of the total visual information. So for videoblogging, high-definition cameras are overkill.

This leaves two ideal choices for videoblogging: DV cameras and digital still cameras that shoot video. These cameras can be purchased for under $500 and work well with today's video-editing software. Let's take a closer look at these options.

DV Video Cameras

Digital Video, or DV, has been the primary format for consumer video cameras since the late 1990s. The big deal about these cameras is that

they record video digitally instead of in an analog format like old VHS and Hi-8 cameras. And DV is easy and inexpensive to transfer to your computer and edit. (In fact, the two editing applications we recommend later in this chapter were specifically designed to capture and edit video from DV cameras.)

Figure 3.1 MiniDV tapes are about the size of a matchbox and hold between 60 and 90 minutes of footage.

In North America, DV cameras shoot an image with a standard frame size of 720 by 480 pixels at a standard frame rate (the number of frames recorded or played back per second) of 30 frames per second, or fps. Most DV cameras record video on MiniDV tapes. These matchbox size tapes hold 60 to 90 minutes of video. And since the tapes are so small, you'll find many DV cameras are small and convenient to carry around (**Figure 3.1**).

All DV cameras connect to a computer via a FireWire cable. So if you'll be using a DV camera, it's important to make sure your computer has a FireWire port. Almost every Mac made since 2001 has come with FireWire built in, but not all PCs do. Check by looking for a port that is

labelled *IEEE 1394*, *FireWire*, *iLink*, or that has the FireWire symbol on it (**Figure 3.2**). FireWire comes in three versions, a 6-pin and a 4-pin port for FireWire 400 (standard) and, for the faster FireWire 800, a 9-pin Port

Figure 3.2   DV cameras connect to computers via a FireWire cable. Check for a FireWire port on your computer by looking for this FireWire symbol or ports labeled IEEE 1394 or iLink.

(**Figure 3.3**). Macs and many PCs have 6-pin ports. A few PCs, especially laptops, have 4-pin ports.

4-pin   6-pin   9-pin

Figure 3.3 On FireWire cables for desktop computers, a 4-pin connector plugs into the DV camera, while the 6-pin connector on the other end plugs into the computer. Only Macs with FireWire 800 ports need 9-pin connectors but they have standard FireWire ports as well.

Moving from Analog to Digital

If you've got a library of old VHS, 8mm, or Hi-8 tapes that you'd like to include in your videoblog, you'll need a way to convert that footage to DV so you can edit it in your computer. To do this, you'll need to have access to some type of analog-to-digital converter. One option is a stand-alone converter box that takes an input from your analog source and has an output that goes directly into your computer via FireWire. One example would be the Canopus ADVC-110, which we found online for as little as $285 (see "Smart Shopping").

You can also find DV cameras that have a similar function, called "pass through," because the signal is passed through the camera directly into the computer and not recorded on the MiniDV tape in the camera. One example includes the Canon ZR100, which we found online for less than $230.

Another option is the Digital8 camera from Sony. This "hybrid" camera records high-resolution DV video on Hi-8 tapes instead of MiniDV tapes. Hybrid cameras were designed to be a bridge for people with a library of Hi-8 and 8mm tapes who wanted to move to DV format. Digital8 cameras can play back the older tapes and send the 8mm or Hi-8 video over FireWire directly into your computer for editing.

If you're in the market for a new DV camera and don't need to capture video from older tapes, you should probably stick with one of the many cameras that record to MiniDV.

If your PC doesn't have a FireWire port, you can probably add one by purchasing and installing an inexpensive FireWire card. If your Mac is so old it doesn't have a FireWire port, adding one will be either expensive or impossible.

Digital Still Cameras

Many videobloggers have begun to use digital still cameras that also shoot video. Lots of digital still cameras can save video clips on their memory cards in the same way they save still images. Some digital photo cameras are even designed to function like a tiny camcorder, with a flip-out LCD view screen and a camcorder-style ergonomic design (**Figure 3.4**). These make shooting video from different angles and getting yourself into the shot much easier.

Figure 3.4

Cameras in the Sanyo Xacti series look and act much like traditional video cameras.

The quality of a still image is measured in megapixels. However, when you shoot video on these cameras, megapixels are not a factor. Video quality depends mostly on frame size and frame rate, measured in frames per second, or fps. The highest quality image available on these cameras is a frame size of 640 by 480 pixels at 30 fps. The lower quality is a frame size of 320 by 240 pixels at 15 fps. That's the frame size you'll ultimately be posting on your videoblog.

The video quality from digital still cameras isn't as good as that of a DV camera, but the difference is marginal once video is prepared for the Web, and there are several advantages to using a digital still camera. One big advantage is the small size. DV cameras are small but some of these photo cameras are downright tiny, the size of a cell phone (**Figure 3.5**). That means they are easy to carry wherever you go.

Figure 3.5

Many digital still cameras, like this tiny Canon PowerShot SD200, also capture video clips.

Another advantage is that digital still cameras don't use tapes. Instead they use a reusable memory card, which means you won't have any last-minute trips to the store to buy a new tape. Finally, transferring video from a memory card to your PC is generally more convenient than transferring video from tapes—but not always. The ease of importing video depends on the computer, editing software, and digital formats you are working with, issues we cover in Chapter 5.

A Checklist for Digital Still Cameras

When purchasing a digital still camera or assessing the one you already own, you'll want to make sure it has the options you'll need for videoblogging. For example, some older or super cheap still cameras shoot video but not sound. Some others capture video and audio but they don't have a speaker on the camera for playback, so you can't audition the sound until you download your videos to your computer. If you don't know if your camera records sound, shoot a short video clip and import it to your computer to make sure it's capable of capturing sound as well as video. Here are additional issues to consider:

Video File Formats. Digital still cameras record video as a file, similar to other computer documents. Depending on your camera, clips will be saved as .avi, .mov, .mp4, or .mpg (short for MPEG) files. These formats are basically containers that hold video and audio information. Picture a jar filled with layers of colored sand. You could put that sand in any container: a Mason jar, a plastic bottle, or a vase. No matter what container you use, the sand is the same. But some containers, or formats, are more compatible in editing than others.

Some digital still cameras, like the Sony CyberShot, capture audio and video in MPEG1, which is a *muxed* format. Muxed means the audio and the video tracks are combined into one, and it's big trouble when you want to edit your video clips. Most editing programs cannot work with either muxed clips or .mpg formats, so try to avoid cameras that record in those formats.

Memory Cards. The storage capacity of a memory card is related to its size. So no matter what kind of memory card a camera uses, bigger is better. If you want to shoot video, you'll need at least a 512 MB memory card, and a 1 GB card is even better. Memory cards are getting cheaper and cheaper these days, so you shouldn't have to break the bank to buy a couple of 512 MB cards or a single 1 GB card (see "Smart Shopping").

Recording Capacity. Depending on your camera's settings and the capacity of its card you'll be able to shoot between 20 minutes and 3 hours of video. The total can vary wildly based on several factors. Lower-quality recording, say 320 by 240 pixels at 15 fps, doesn't gobble up as much card space as a higher-quality setting, say 640 by 480 pixels at 30 fps. So the frame size and fps rate greatly affect how much footage you can shoot.

The file format your camera shoots in will also affect how much footage you can shoot. For example, Canon PowerShot cameras shoot in .avi. With a 1 GB card, they can hold only 40 minutes of video when set at 320 by 240 pixels at 15 fps. In contrast, the Sanyo Xacti camera records in .mp4 and can shoot 230 minutes of video at that same setting. You'll have to play with the settings on your particular camera to find the balance between quality and recording capacity that's right for you.

Video Clip Length. Another thing to take into account is the length of each video clip you can record. Some cameras will let you record continuously until their memory card is filled. Others limit each recording to a predetermined length such as 30 seconds or 3 minutes. Don't overlook this if you're buying a new camera.

Retro Style

Some of the older digital still cameras that save images to floppy discs, like the Sony Mavica MVC FD-83, record decent .mov clips with sound.

Smart Shopping

Comparing cameras online can often save you time and money. Try http://shopping.yahoo.com and http://froogle.google.com for comparison shopping.

If you're strapped for cash but in the market for a video camera, don't forget to consider the cost of the tapes you'll need for shooting compared to the one-time cost of memory cards for digital still cameras.

Finally, the least expensive cameras run on AA batteries and practically eat them for breakfast, especially when shooting video. Unless you have a system of always having fresh or rechargeable AA batteries, these cameras are going to leave you in a lurch when shooting (and it never fails that the batteries will die right in the middle of that all-important shot). Lithium rechargeable (Li-Ion) batteries are more expensive than disposables but are worth the investment. They hold a charge for hours and will last for years.

If you plan to use one of these for vlogging, expect some geek-style street credibility for your cool retro technology.

But remember, having a camera that shoots video is more important than the kind of camera you have. As we've mentioned, some cameras are much easier to use for vlogging than others. But as long as you can transfer the footage from your camera to your computer for editing and uploading to the Web, you can vlog—whether you use a tiny digital still, a brand-new DV camcorder, or an elderly Hi-8.

Editing Software

Once you've shot your video, you will need editing software to import the video into your computer. Video editing has never been easier. Your PC or Mac probably arrived with a great piece of video editing software with everything you need to get started. If not, or if you simply want more choices, there are editing programs for everyone from beginners to Hollywood pros.

Apple's iMovie

Hands down the easiest and least expensive way to edit video on a Mac is with iMovie HD, which is part of Apple's iLife suite of applications. If you're using OS X, some version of iMovie is probably sitting on your Mac already. There are many nice things about iMovie HD compared to the original iMovie, including improved editing tools, better integration with the other iLife applications (including iTunes, iDVD, iPhoto, and Garageband), and support for the new HDV (high definition video) format. Make sure you have the latest version, which at this writing is iMovie HD 6.0. If you already have iMovie HD, you can download the latest upgrade at www.apple.com/ilife/imovie. If you don't have iMovie HD, you can purchase it as part of the iLife '06 suite at www.apple.com/ilife.

To check which version of iMovie you have, launch iMovie and choose iMovie > About iMovie. A window will appear with the version number (Figure 3.6).

Figure 3.6

Windows Movie Maker

Windows XP comes with its own free and easy-to-use video editor called Windows Movie Maker. If you haven't run the Windows Service Pack 2 update mentioned in Chapter 1, do it now so you'll also get the latest version of Movie Maker, which at this writing is 2.1. While you're at it, download the Creativity Fun Pack. It's free and features extra titles, music, and sound effects good for spicing up your videoblog. You can download Windows Movie Maker and Creativity Fun Pack at www.microsoft.com/windowsxp/downloads/powertoys/mmcreate.mspx.

To check which version of Windows Movie Maker you have, launch Windows Movie Maker and choose Help > About Windows Movie Maker. A window will appear with the version number (**Figure 3.7**).

Figure 3.7
Check here to see which version of Movie Maker your PC is using.

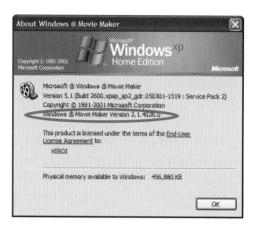

More Sophisticated Options

iMovie and Windows Movie Maker are entry-level editing applications that are the most popular and cheapest choices for videobloggers. For a price, several other editing applications offer additional bells and whistles. For PC users they include Premiere Elements and Premier Pro from Adobe and Vegas Movie Studio and Vegas 6.0 from Sony. For Mac users they include Final Cut Express and Final Cut Pro from Apple (www.apple.com). Avid (www.avid.com) has a variety of professional editing applications that can be used on Mac or PC. The price for these programs varies from $100 to several thousand, but you can sample several editors for free. Download trial versions of

- Adobe Premiere Elements and Premiere Pro at www.adobe.com/products/tryadobe/main.jsp

- Sony's Vegas Movie Studio and Vegas 6.0 at www.sonymediasoftware.com/download/step1.asp?CatID=1

You can pay thousands of dollars for editing software but free programs like iMovie and Windows Movie Maker are fine for vlogging. As long as a program lets you easily import and edit video for use on the Web, you're all set.

Music and Sound

It's been said that good audio makes your video look better. It's true. One easy way to create a certain mood for your video is to add some music. The bad news is that none of the great music in your CD collection can be used in your videos. All the songs and music contained on those CDs are copyrighted and can't be used unless you obtain a license that allows you to distribute a particular song on the Internet as part of your videoblog. A license can cost thousands of dollars. That's the bad news. The good news is that there are plenty of snappy tunes available for you to use free of charge. In this section we'll look at where to find free music for your vlog, two applications that help you create your own music, and a few professional options for sound fanatics.

Creative Commons Music

As we mentioned in Chapter 2, Creative Commons is helpful to vloggers because it provides flexible copyright licenses for creative works. Many musicians have copyrighted their work under these licenses as well and will let you use their music for free, as long as you use it for nonprofit purposes and follow any other terms of the license (**Figure 3.8**).

Figure 3.8

ccMixter.org is one of several great directories of free music and audio samples available for you to use thanks to generous creators and Creative Commons.

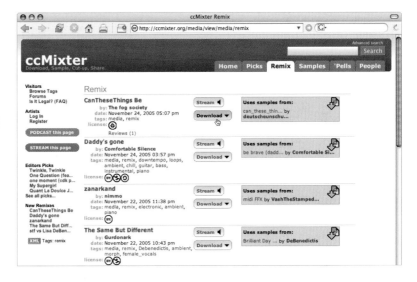

More Music

These sites are also terrific sources for free music copyrighted under licenses from Creative Commons:

- http://ccmixter.org/

- http://magnatune.com/

- www.opsound.org/

- www.soundclick.com/

- http://freesound.iua.upf.edu/

Some musicians use licenses that basically let you use an entire song, as long as you give them credit. Others say you may help yourself to a sample, but only a sample, of a musical work. Terms vary so check them carefully before you actually add any Creative Commons-licensed music to your vlog.

Audacity

http://audacity.sourceforge.net

If you want to add a single voice or music track to your videos, iMovie and Movie Maker can handle the job. But if you'd like to create new music using samples or you'd like to remove hiss or hum that's present in the audio in your videos, you'll need something else. The favorite free tool for this is Audacity, a great audio editor that works on both PCs and Macs (**Figure 3.9**).

Figure 3.9

Audacity makes it easy to edit audio on both PCs and Macs. Best of all, this program is free!

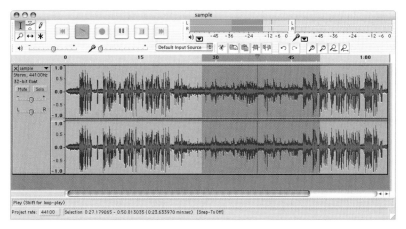

GarageBand (Mac only)

www.apple.com/ilife/garageband

If you have a Mac with iLife, you also have a great program to create royalty-free music for your videoblogs. GarageBand comes with 1GB of audio loops and additional sound loops can be purchased from Apple (**Figure 3.10**). One of GarageBand's nice features is that it keeps all of the loops in time with each other. That means you can create interesting music even if you don't have much of an ear for the finer points of composition. If you are a musician—heck, even if you're not—you can hook GarageBand up to a USB keyboard (which runs under $100 for a cheap version), compose your own melody, and add lots of great tracks to it.

Promote Local Talent

Did you see a great jazz show on Friday night at a local club? Does your best friend's electro-pop quintet rock? Ask for written permission to use their music in videos for your vlog (go back to Chapter 2 for details). This is a great way to add a unique touch to your projects while simultaneously promoting local, independent musicians.

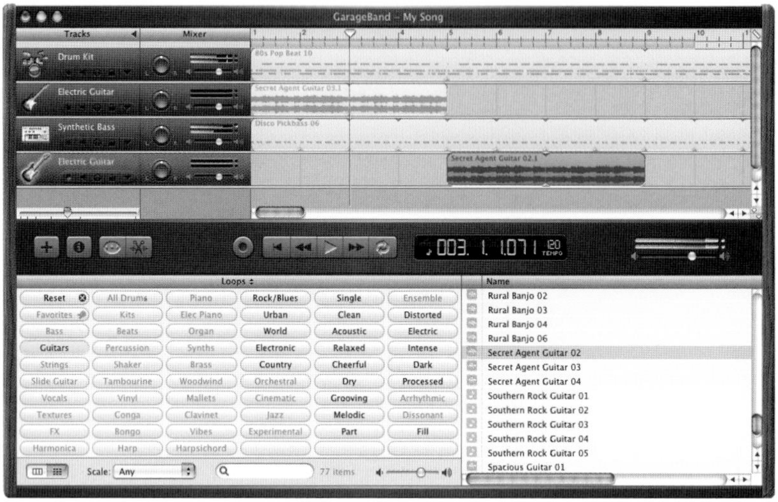

Figure 3.10

GarageBand comes with hundreds of pre-recorded audio loops that make music creation super fun and easy.

Other Sound Options

You may already know that there's a host of advanced software designed for sound professionals. These include Apple's Soundtrack Pro, Logic Express, and Logic as well as Avid's ProTools. You can find out more at www.apple.com and www.avid.com, respectively.

Expensive sound and editing programs may be fun but they're not necessary to have in your toolbox. We've said it before and we'll say it again: You don't need sophisticated tools for successful vlogging.

Shooting Video

In this chapter we'll take a look at some of the things you need to consider before shooting video for your vlog, such as creating a plan, determining the length of your finished piece, and ensuring that you record usable video and audio. Because your clips will need to be compressed, or reduced in size, to be posted on the Web, we'll give you some insight on how compression can affect video quality. We'll also show you easy ways to make your videos look and sound good enough that they won't distract viewers from the most important thing—what you have to say.

If you're an experienced cameraperson or filmmaker, you may want to enlist the help of a crew or use additional equipment to give your videos a more polished look. But this isn't a competition, and you don't need to be a video pro to start shooting.

Getting Started

Now that you've visited a lot of vlogs, you may have gotten the idea that videobloggers tend to be pretty spontaneous when it comes to video production. If so, you're right. Sometimes all the planning a vlogger needs for a shoot is to make sure there's a charged battery in the camera. In other situations, an actual plan can be helpful.

Making a Plan

Before you start shooting, you should know what your subject matter is, where the story will take place, and who you want on camera to tell the story. For a simple video, that may be all the planning needed. If you want to produce a more complex video, a more detailed plan may make shooting go smoother. Sketching out a plan can be the key to successfully realizing your vision.

Don't let the idea of planning intimidate you. A plan can as simple as a few notes for a voice-over that you want to record after you've shot your footage. Or it can be a scripted dialog between different people . It can also be an improvisational guide with suggestions of what might happen in a given scene (**Figure 4.1**). A plan is pretty much whatever

Figure 4.1

A plan doesn't have to be complicated. The plan for Michael's video "NODE101:: San Antonio Intro" is a short list of points he and a fellow vlogger wanted to share with viewers. You can see the result at http://michaelverdi. com/index.php/2005/ 10/24/node101-intro.

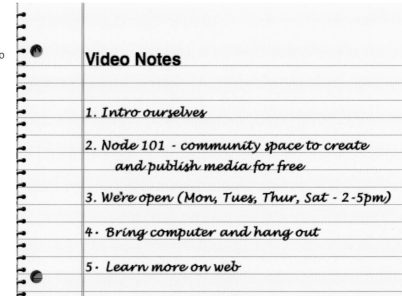

Video Notes

1. Intro ourselves

2. Node 101 - community space to create
      and publish media for free

3. We're open (Mon, Tues, Thur, Sat - 2-5pm)

4. Bring computer and hang out

5. Learn more on web

you need it to be, as long as it serves your creative process. A clear plan can help eliminate anxiety over the universal artists' question: Is this going to turn out the way I see it in my head?

Creating a Storyboard

Another way of creating a plan for your video is to sketch out its scenes. You may have heard about *storyboarding* a script. It's a term used in film production for the process in which scenes are literally drawn on paper, like comic strips, to show how they will look for each camera angle (**Figure 4.2**). Storyboarding can get tedious if you plan on creating a really long video, but it can be a lot of fun to sketch out the possibilities. Storyboarding is a good tool when you need to make the most of your production time and energy.

Figure 4.2
A storyboard doesn't have to look like a work of art. Stick figures will get the job done.

note Don't let the idea of planning overwhelm or intimidate you, or stop you from being spontaneous. The unplanned events or actions that happen during a shoot often turn out great.

Keeping it Short

"Keep it short" should become your mantra. It's best to limit the videos for your vlog to five minutes or less. In fact, keeping your videos under three minutes is probably ideal for both you and your audience.

First, the more footage you shoot, the longer it'll take you to edit. If you shoot about two minutes of raw footage for each minute of a finished video (a reasonable ratio), you'll actually be able to complete a video project sometime before the end of this century—if you keep it short. Remember, you want videoblogging to become a *part* of your life, not your *entire* life.

Short is sweet for your audience too. Watching video on a computer is not the same as watching TV while lounging on a couch. Your audience will probably have many other things begging for their attention, like an urgent email or a spreadsheet that has to be crunched by 5 PM. Albert Einstein, who was a pretty smart guy, once said, "Make everything as simple as possible, but no simpler." He was probably talking about physics, but that's good advice for videoblogs, too.

Working with Your Camera

There are two basic ways to shoot with your camera. One way to shoot is by holding the camera in your hands. This gives you the ability to set up quickly and move with the action if necessary. The other way is to put the camera on a tripod. A tripod is invaluable when you need a stable image but it also restricts how easily you can move the camera. You also have to carry the darn thing around.

We prefer the more mobile approach, which allows for things like getting an interview while walking down the street. Holding your camera doesn't cost any money or require extra gear that takes up space in your backpack. There is a drawback to shooting handheld, though. With small DV cameras and tiny digital still cameras, it's easy to end up with shaky footage that looks like it was taken in the middle of an earthquake. But your shots don't have to be shaky. You can experiment with different camera grips to see what works best, but we recommend cradling the camera in your open palms. Try moving the camera fluidly, as though you're doing Tai Chi. This technique can produce pretty smooth shots, with practice. There are other ways to minimize the "shaky cam" effect as well, which we discuss below.

Facing Forward

If you need to walk and shoot video at the same time, face forward. That's our most important piece of advice for avoiding the shakes. People often shoot while walking sideways or backwards. That can cause you to trip, have an accident, or drop your camera. Also, walking sideways or backwards can increase the shakiness of your shooting. So always face forward. Move the camera, not your body, to shoot the action. (Using the flip-out LCD screen, if your camera has one, will make that easier to do.) Facing forward is the best (and safest) way to produce smooth-looking video.

Steady Shots with Digital Still Cameras

If you're shooting with a digital still camera that doesn't have a rotating LCD screen, you can overcome shaky footage with a little practice. You'll need to face forward while walking and hold your camera as we've described above. Then you need to make your best guess about what is in frame and what is out. That's where the practice comes in.

Enlist some friends to help you do a few test runs with your camera to get a sense of how to aim your shots. Over time you'll learn how to shoot on the go without making your audience seasick.

Shooting Sideways

If you want to videotape a person walking next to you, you'll need to flip your camera's LCD screen around so that it faces outward but is still flush against the side of the camera. Then cradle the camera in your upturned hands and position it parallel to your body so that the lens faces your subject and you can view the LCD screen (**Figure 4.3**).

Figure 4.3 Here's how you can record someone walking by your side.

When shooting this way, it's important to find a comfortable position for holding the camera. You'll need to keep your arms loose but fairly close to your body. The further you extend your arms, the heavier your camera will feel. It's helpful to think of your arms as shock absorbers. If the camera has a handle on top of it and feels awkward in your upturned hands, you can try suspending it from one hand by the handle. This position lets the camera "float" as you walk.

Taping Yourself with Another Person

Getting yourself into a shot with your subject is a little trickier, but it can be done. Open the camera's LCD screen completely, so it's at a right angle to the camera body, as shown in **Figure 4.4**. Now hold the camera in front and away from your body, almost at arm's length. Use the LCD screen to line up the shot. Try to "memorize" the position of your arm for the shot so you can watch where you are going instead of keeping your eyes on the camera. The slight angle created by holding the camera out in front should be enough to place you and the person walking next to you in the frame.

Figure 4.4 Here's how you can capture yourself and your subject in a walking shot.

> **note** You might notice in the above examples that the LCD screen shows a reversed image, which is typical of many DV cameras when you're shooting in this position.

Shooting Behind You

You can videotape people behind you with nearly the same technique you used for shooting to the side. Start by flipping out the LCD screen and swiveling it to face in the same direction as the camera lens. Now hold the camera in front and slightly to one side of your body. Point the lens behind you, toward the person you want to shoot (**Figure 4.5**). Now you can shoot while walking forward, which is much easier than trying to shoot and walk backward. And you can monitor the video image from time to time in the LCD screen.

Figure 4.5 Videotape people behind you by pointing the camera toward them and off to the side.

Shooting Yourself

The previous position can also be adapted for the classic "talking to the camera" videoblogger shot. Once again, the camera should be in front of you, either directly or off to the side. Remember to look at the lens and not at the LCD screen so you are talking directly to your viewer. (**Figure 4.6**)

Figure 4.6 These images show how to capture the classic videoblogger shot: talking directly to the camera.

Lighting Your Video

Without enough light your video will look like mud, it's as simple as that. So it's really important to have enough light when you're shooting. But you don't want too much light, either. You can't control every shooting situation, but you can make the best of whatever light is available with our tips below.

Indoor Shooting

If you're shooting inside, it probably won't hurt to turn on all the lights in the room. If you can, arrange the light sources so that they point to your subject and are beside the camera. You don't have to rearrange furniture (especially if it's not your house), but you may want to move your subject to accommodate the available light.

One common mistake is to have a subject face the camera with his back to the light source. When the light behind him enters the lens, your camera tries to compensate for the disparity in light between the subject and the light source. But it can't, so you often end up with a silhouette instead of a recognizable person (**Figure 4.7**).

Figure 4.7
In the image on the left, the light is directly behind the subject. Position the light source in front and to the side of the subject for better results.

A light directly over a subject can also create problems, such as harsh shadows on the person's head or face (**Figure 4.8**). To remedy this, move the subject a few feet to the side, out of the direct path of the light. That way your subject can catch any light that's being reflected from the floor, ceiling, or wall. You can also position a subject near a window to use daylight as a lighting source. Position yourself and the camera near the window, facing your subject. Don't let the subject stand between the camera and the window, or you'll end up with another silhouette.

Figure 4.8
Overhead light creates extreme shadows. Move the subject, or the light, for higher quality images.

Outdoor Shooting

Several of the principles that apply to shooting inside, also apply to shooting outside. For example, never position your subject's back toward the sun. Once again, your camera will try to compensate for that big ball of fire shining directly at it and turn your subject into a silhouette. On the other hand, you have to be careful when facing people toward the sun. You don't want them to have to squint to keep from being blinded.

Another common mistake is to shoot with your subject partly in the shade and partly in the sun. Your camera will try to compensate and end up making the shady part too dark or the sunlit part too bright. Often, what works best is to find a nice shady place out of the direct sunlight (**Figure 4.9**).

Figure 4.9
The image on the left shows the harshness of direct sunlight. Indirect light can create a much smoother, more attractive image.

Framing Your Shots

Framing is what you do when you zoom in or adjust the camera's position to select the size and placement of your subject within the viewfinder. You probably have an intuitive sense of how framing works from watching TV and movies, and you may be familiar with basic shots. But since your video is destined for the Web rather than Hollywood, let's review framing and shots with a videoblog in mind.

You can move closer or farther from your subject in two ways: by zooming in and out with the camera lens, and by physically moving the camera. These two methods produce slightly different results. The close-up shown in **Figure 4.10** was shot at a distance by zooming in on the subject. The close-up in **Figure 4.11** was shot with the camera at arm's length from the subject. Notice how the background in the first close-up is out of focus, while the background in the second is in focus. Both close ups keep our attention where the vlogger wants it, on the subjects being taped.

Figure 4.10 In this close up from "Segue (Hiatus)," a video from his Taxiplasm Vlog about high school graduation, Brian Gonzalez zooms in from a distance to blur the background and focus our attention on a friend. http://guitseretni. blogspot.com/2005/ 06/segue-hiatus.html

Figure 4.11 In this close-up from Chris Weagel's "LAC St. Clair" from the Human Dog Laboratory vlog, the camera is zoomed out but close to the subject's face, which keeps the background in focus. www.human-dog.com/lab/?p=62

The opposite of the close-up is the wide shot. Use wide shots to establish the location of your subject, capture a lot of action, or follow someone moving quickly. To shoot a true wide shot, you need to both position your camera far from the subject or scene and zoom out. In **Figure 4.12**, Sara Weagel uses a wide shot to establish that she's practicing alone on a soccer field

Figure 4.12

In this wide shot, the viewer can see Sara Weagel alone on the field as she practices her game in "Oh Boy, Soccer!" from her vlog, Sara's Corner. www. human-dog.com/sara/ ?p=17

In a videoblog, wide shots like Sara's are best used for only a few seconds at a time. That's because once the video is resized for the Web, a distant figure will be extremely small and hard to see. Longer wide shots can work on the Web if whatever fills the frame is the main attraction. The mountain scene shot during Josh Leo's hike in Germany is a good example (**Figure 4.13**).

Figure 4.13

In "German Hiking Part 2," from Josh Leo's Vlog, Josh uses a wide shot to show us the view while hiking in the Bavarian Alps. http://joshleo.blogspot. com/2005/11/german- hiking-part-2.html

In the medium shot, your subject is still prominent but viewers can also see where the action is taking place or what's around your subject. In **Figure 4.14**, Charlene Rule uses a medium shot to show us the excitement of a friend just moments before she is married, and the rush of activity around her.

Figure 4.14 In "Vero Strut" from Charlene Rule's vlog Scratch Video, Charlene films her friend strutting down a back hallway on her way to the altar.

In the same video, Charlene uses a two-shot to capture a moment she shared with a friend (**Figure 4.15**).

Figure 4.15
A few seconds later Charlene and her friend share a laugh.

Some vloggers use a variety of shots within a single video, while others just use one or two. Television and film have stylistic rules about which shot to use when, but as a vlogger you have a slightly different set of visual concerns—namely the small viewing size and short length of your video. So before you start recording, ask yourself how you can frame your scenes so they translate effectively onto the (really) small screen.

Recording Clear Audio

Sound makes all the difference when it comes to shooting good quality video, so it's important to get the best audio recording possible. You may have a beautiful shot lined up but if the audio is noisy and unintelligible, you're going to be cursing the video gods for eternity. Here are some basic rules for recording good, clean audio.

For best results, the ideal solution is to invest in a decent external microphone that attaches to your camera (**Figure 4.16**). External mics come in all sizes and prices. Some microphones can be attached to the camera, while other, smaller mics (sometimes called lavalier or tie-clip mics) can be attached to your subject's clothing.

Figure 4.16

An external microphone, such as the Sony ECM-MS908C Stereo mic, can help guarantee quality sound for less than $100.

When using an external microphone, wear headphones to monitor the sound quality and sound level coming into the camera. Before you start recording audio, have your subject speak clearly towards the microphone to test that it is working and that you are recording clean, audible sound. If your mic runs on batteries, keep a spare set on hand, and replace them whenever the signal gets weak.

While an external microphone will produce the best audio, the little microphones built into video cameras, and even digital still cameras (**Figure 4.17**) can do a pretty good job if they are positioned next to the person talking. If you don't want to carry around an external mic, or your camera doesn't have a microphone input jack, make sure you get as close as possible to your subject.

Figure 4.17
If you're using a small digital camera, there is no way to connect an external microphone. For better audio, get the internal mic close to your subject.

If you can arrange it, try to shoot somewhere quiet. Instead of interviewing your mayor on a busy street outside city hall, for example, see if you can do it inside his or her office. Also, don't be afraid to interrupt recording to let a truck pass by. When its time to start editing, you'll be glad you did.

Considering Compression

In Chapter 6 you'll learn about compressing video for the Web. To get the best quality compressed video, it's good to keep a few things in mind while you shoot. Basically, the more detail in a shot and the more a shot changes from frame to frame (because of fast editing or lots of motion), the more difficult it will be to produce good-looking compressed images.

For example, a smooth tripod-shot of a person talking in front of a plain white wall will look great after compression. But a hand-held shot of someone running through a forest may look awful as a compressed file. Don't let compression dictate the kind of video you shoot, just be conscious of it. If you have a choice and can avoid shots with lots of motion and detail and still make the video you want to make, you'll end up with better results. (**Figures 4.18** and **4.19** show what happens when you don't have a choice.)

Figure 4.18 This uncompressed video image is clear and detailed.

Figure 4.19 The compressed Web version of the same image is blurry and has less detail.

You should also watch for stripes and unfriendly patterns when you shoot. Many video cameras have a hard time recording complex patterns like plaid or compact stripes. The patterns may appear to bleed together, or you may see a shimmer along the lines, creating a moiré pattern. This is why television anchors rarely wear pinstripes, checks, or complex patterns. Don't let this problem deter you. Again, just be aware that translating a certain amount of detail in a satisfactory way may not always be possible.

Editing for Vlogs

Twenty-five years ago or so, a single editing station could cost more than $250,000. Today you can get real editing power for free with programs like Windows Movie Maker and Apple's iMovie. The award-winning documentary "Tarnation," for example, which is kind of like a 90-minute videoblog, was edited entirely in iMovie and was the first such movie to gain theatrical distribution.

Whether you're editing a feature film or a vlog, the basic principle of editing holds true: You want to choose the best shots to tell your story or convey your concept, then arrange them in an order that holds meaning for you. In this chapter, we cover the editing process as it relates particularly to vlogging, no matter what your story is or what application you use. You can find step-by-step instructions for using iMovie or Movie Maker in their built-in Help tools, various online resources, and books like Peachpit's Visual QuickStart and Visual

QuickProject Guides. This chapter guides you through the overall process of telling a story with video.

Getting Started

We talked in Chapter 4 about framing shots. Wide shots are usually used to establish context, because they show more information about where your subject is physically located than close-up shots. Close-ups, on the other hand, are good for revealing something about your subject's character or emotions. Sometimes you need a variety of shots to tell a story, but sometimes you don't. If you choose to capture your whole story in one shot, for example, your editing workload is going to be pretty light. The videos shown in **Figures 5.1** and **5.2** illustrate the extremes of video editing. Though they're very different, the story of each video is clearly defined.

Figure 5.1 Eric Nelson is a professional basketball player. In "The Knee Year," he uses footage shot over the course of a year to explore his journey from knee surgery, through rehab, to playing in a game again. You can find it at http://bottomunion.com/blog/?p=117

Figure 5.2 "Brooklyn Snow Storm," at http://www.scratchvideo.tv/scratch/2006/02/brooklyn_snow_s.html began as a single 30-minute video shot, which was then speeded up in editing so that it all elapses in one minute.

The first step of editing is to view your footage and decide which portions define or shape the story. If you started out with a plan, when you edit you will arrange your shots according to your notes, script, or storyboard. Sometimes the story that you shot is not exactly the story that you planned. Either something completely unexpected happened or things just didn't quite turn out the way you thought they would. This isn't a bad thing. Editing is a magical process. It's often the unexpected shot that turns out to be the gem of a piece.

Videos for vlogs are generally pretty short, so part of the shaping process is trimming material you don't need so your audience sees just the good stuff. Review your footage with several questions in mind. Does a particular shot move the story forward or give the audience important information? If not, you'll want to set that shot aside. Are there two shots that tell viewers the same thing? Maybe you can cut one out to move the story along more quickly. Remember, you're not making *The Godfather*; you don't have 10 minutes to establish the setting, time period, and main characters before getting to the main story.

As you trim the fat and focus your story, you'll be selecting and organizing specific shots into a sequence that flows together. This is where you'll use wide shots, close-ups, and medium shots to tell your story in a way that makes sense. All the while, especially if you're new to working with video, you'll notice how things might fit together better if they'd been shot a little differently. There's a symbiotic relationship between shooting and editing. Learning how to edit will make you a better shooter, and becoming a better shooter will make editing easier. The really great thing about this process is that you're constantly learning and becoming a better storyteller.

Unlimited Editing Options

Computer-based editing software allows for nonlinear, nondestructive editing. This means you can position your video clips in any order and rearrange that order at any time, giving you virtually unlimited editing options. If you're not happy with the way your video is turning out, you can easily try another approach.

Preparing Your Footage

Before you can actually begin editing, you have to import the video footage from your camera into your computer. You can capture one long chunk of video and break it down into smaller bits within the editing application. Or you can view the footage but choose to capture only those shots you know you want to use. Once the footage has been imported, you'll need to collect any other material you'll want to add to your video, such as music or still images. But before you do anything else, it's a good idea to get organized.

Organizing Your Files

Since video files take up a lot of disc space, it's important to get organized before you import footage to your computer. We recommend keeping all files related to a particular video project together in one folder (**Figures 5.3, 5.4**). Once you've finished a project, you'll find a single folder easy to back up and easy to remove from your hard drive to free up more space for the next project (See "Backing Up Your Files").

Figure 5.3

Simplify your videoblogging by using one folder for all the files related to a single project. If you use a Mac, put the folder under Movies to make it easy to find.

Figure 5.4

If you use a PC, put your project folder in the My Videos folder so it won't get lost.

Backing Up Your Files

The problem with video files is that they're huge, and while hard drives are getting cheaper all the time, space doesn't grow on trees. Sooner or later you're going to need to delete finished projects from your drive to make room for new ones.

If you are using a DV camera, your best bet is to keep your original source tapes and don't reuse them. Also, exporting a copy of your edited project back to tape is a good idea. This way you'll have a pristine copy of all of your hard work.

Obviously, if you are shooting video with a digital still camera, you have to do something else. Instead of exporting a copy back to tape, you can save a DV version of your edited project to your hard drive as a file. You can then take that DV file and your original camera clips and burn them to a DVD. This archive DVD won't play back the way a DVD that you watch in your living room will. The files will be stored on the DVD in the same format as on your hard drive. A single-layer data DVD can hold 4.7GB of information, good for about 20 minutes of DV video. Many new DVD burners use dual-layer discs, which, you guessed it, store twice as much.

For more information on exporting your project back to tape or as a DV file on your hard drive, see your editing program's Help files.

If your computer doesn't have a DVD burner you might consider purchasing an external one that connects via FireWire or USB 2.0. A DVD burner will set you back $100 to $150.

Importing Video from DV Cameras

To capture DV video from your camera, you will need to connect it to your computer with a FireWire cable. (Some cameras come with these cables, but if yours didn't, you'll need to buy one separately.) As we mentioned in Chapter 3, the smaller 4-pin connector plugs into the port on your camera and the larger, 6-pin connector plugs into a desktop computer (**Figure 5.5**). Many Windows-based laptops have 4-pin connectors, so be sure to check first before you buy.

Once you have the cable you need, connect your camera to your computer. To save yourself some frustration, make sure you turn on your camera (in VCR mode) before launching your editing software. Otherwise, the software may not recognize the camera is connected.

Figure 5.5

The 4-pin FireWire connector.

When you have everything connected and turned on, it's time to create your first video project. If you're using iMovie, choose DV when the program prompts you to create a project with a specific video format (**Figure 5.6**). If you're using Windows Movie Maker, the Video Capture Wizard will walk you through the capture process. Simply select DV-AVI as the Digital device format when it prompts you for a Video Setting (**Figure 5.7**).

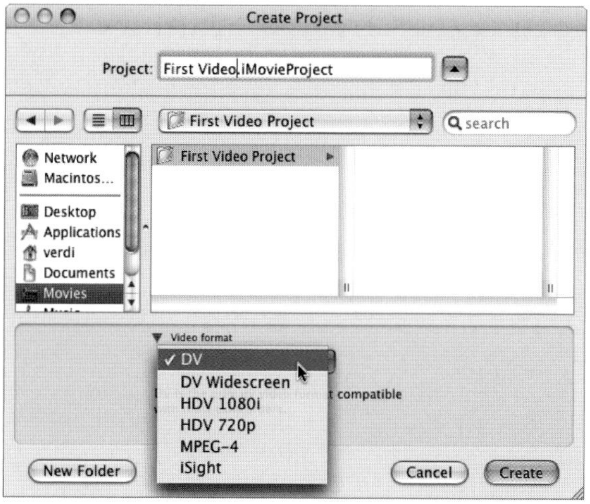

Figure 5.6

If you're using iMovie, choose DV as the video format for your project.

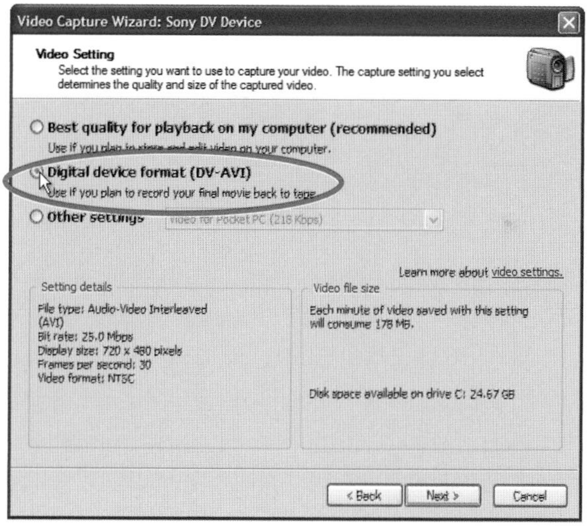

Figure 5.7

If you're using Windows Moving Maker, choose Digital device format (DV-AVI) when prompted for a Video Setting.

Like most other editing programs, both iMovie and Movie Maker have a capture tool with VCR-like buttons that control your camera remotely. This allows you to view footage from your camera and cue the tape to the location where you want to begin capturing. You can capture one clip at a time or an entire tape. (When deciding how much to import, keep in mind that about four and a half minutes of DV footage takes up about 1 GB of hard drive space as a digital file.)

As you capture footage, make sure you include a few seconds on either side of the shots you plan to use in editing. These extra seconds, called *handles*, may be needed during editing to create transitions in or out of shots. Once you finish capturing all the shots for your project, you'll see that files called clips have been placed in a *bin* for you. The bins used by iMovie and Movie Maker (**Figures 5.8** and **5.9**) look different but accomplish the same task by breaking the footage into smaller, more manageable chunks.

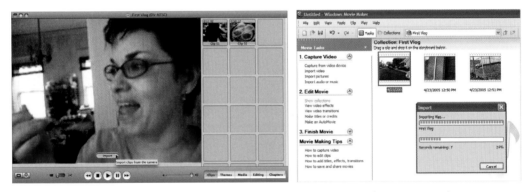

iMovie   *Windows Movie Maker*

Figures 5.8 and 5.9 Both iMovie (left) and Movie Maker (right) can place individual clips in a bin as they import footage.

In traditional film editing, the good takes of a scene were literally cut out of the film and hooked on a rack that hung over a canvas-covered bin. Computer-based editing involves a similar task of choosing and organizing selected clips, and the term bin has been adopted by video editors.

Importing Video from Digital Still Cameras

One day soon importing video from digital still cameras will be a snap—at least, we hope it will be. Today the process can be a little time consuming, depending on the video format your camera saves and the computer and editing application you're using. But don't let that scare you. For many vloggers, the small size and nifty memory cards of these cameras make up for any video-capture quirks. Keep reading for details.

Importing to a Mac

If you use a Mac, connect your camera, and either the software that came with your camera or iPhoto will launch. If you are using iPhoto, click the import button and it will transfer and organize both the photos and the video clips from your camera. Then all you have to do is launch iMovie, create a new DV project and just select all the video clips that you need in iPhoto and drag them to the iMovie project window (**Figure 5.10**). No matter whether your camera saves video in, .mov, .avi, or .mp4, iMovie will convert them all to DV so you can edit them. The downside is that this conversion process can take a long time. The good news is that you can go get yourself a sandwich while this is going on.

note If you're not using iPhoto, check the camera's software documentation for specifics on how and where your files will be transferred.

Figure 5.10

If you use a Mac, you can drag-and-drop video clips from iPhoto to iMovie to edit digital still camera clips. Just don't expect to do it in a hurry.

Importing to a PC

When you connect your camera to your PC and turn it on, the software that came with your camera or the Windows Scanner and Camera Wizard will launch and provide a way to transfer your clips to your computer. Please see the camera's software documentation for specifics on how and where your files will be transferred. If you're using the Wizard be sure to click the Advanced Users Only link (**Figure 5.11**) and drag the clips manually to your video project folder, otherwise the Wizard will skip all of your video files and import only your photos.

Figure 5.11 Clicking the Advanced Users Only link will open up a folder where your clips are stored on your digital still camera.

With your clips in your video project folder, you are ready to get started with Movie Maker. If your camera saves clips as .avi files, you've got it easy. You just import the clips directly from your project folder using the File > Import into Collections command—no conversion necessary (**Figure 5.12**).

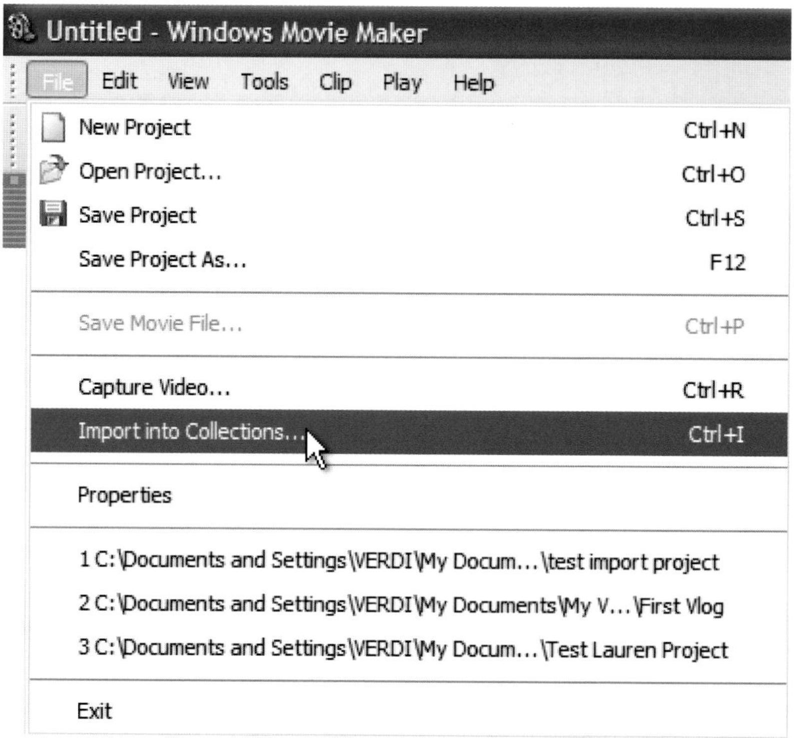

Figure 5.12 Import .avi files into Movie Maker by choosing File > Import into Collections, or by using the keyboard command (Ctrl+I). Then just choose the videos you copied to your project folder to import them.

If your camera saves clips as .mp4 or .mov, you need to convert them to .avi before you can import them. You can download a free program to do this for you called MP4Cam2AVI Easy Convert at http://sourceforge.net/projects/mp4cam2avi/. It's an extra step, but it only takes a few seconds for each clip.

Once you import your digital still clips into Movie Maker, click the Collections Button to see all of your clips (**Figure 5.13**).

Figure 5.13

Clicking the Collections button allows you to browse the clips imported from your digital still camera.

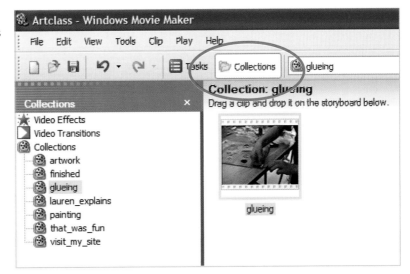

Splitting Your Clips

If the imported footage is in fairly long clips, you'll need to split them into shorter clips before you start editing. To do this, choose a clip and review it. Decide where in the clip you want the next clip to begin. In iMovie choose Edit > Split Video Clip at Playhead (**Figure 5.14**). In Movie Maker choose Clip > Split. Now choose the next clip and do it again. This will turn your big clips into smaller, discrete clips that you'll be able to arrange in any order you want in the timeline.

 In some editing applications, the process of identifying the usable part of a clip is referred to as marking a clip.

 As you go through the process of splitting clips, you might be tempted to delete things you don't think you'll use. Instead, set them aside because there's a chance they could come in handy (see "Don't Delete Potential Gems").

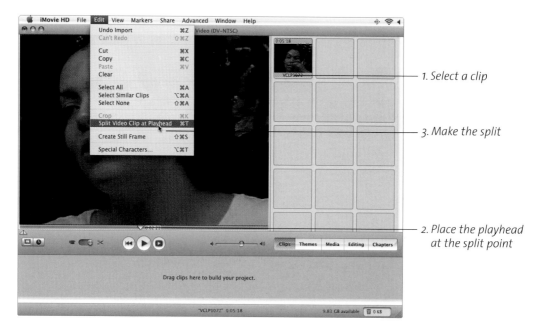

1. Select a clip

3. Make the split

2. Place the playhead at the split point

Figure 5.14 Splitting a clip follows the same process in both iMovie (shown here) and Windows Movie Maker.

Before you start the actual editing, it might be helpful to give your short clips descriptive names instead of the generic ones assigned by your editing program. This is especially useful if you're editing an interview and all of your clips have nearly identical icons (**Figure 5.15**).

Figure 5.15
Give your clips names that will help you remember what part of the story they tell.

thoughts on performing

mic didn't work

it all worked out

Don't Delete Potential Gems

When splitting, renaming, and organizing clips, remember not to delete your extra footage. At times you'll need a little something extra to add to a sequence and, odds are you'll find it in the leftover footage. In her first video, for example, Michael's daughter, Dylan, gives a virtual tour of what it's like to be her. The video was originally intended to end after Dylan looked into the camera and said, "This is Dylan...Goodbye!" But just after she finished the scene, the 11-year-old caught a glimpse of herself in the camera's viewscreen. She wrinkled her nose and said, "Aw, I hate my smile" (**Figure 5.16**). That unexpected moment of self-scrutiny turned out to be the real ending of the video and definitely worth saving!

Figure 5.16

Leftover footage provided a charming and unexpected ending for 11 year-old Dylan Verdi's first video.

Crafting a Rough Cut

Now that you've got all your clips collected and organized, it's time to put together a rough cut. A rough cut is just that—a rough assembly of the shots you want to use sequenced together. You create a rough cut by dragging each clip into the timeline in the order you want it to appear (**Figure 5.17**). Now watch what you've created and ask yourself three questions:

- Is the story all there?

- Does it make sense?

- Are the clips in the best order?

If the answer to any question is no, adjust your rough cut until the answer is yes.

Figure 5.17

A rough cut consists of clips without transitions or effects, as shown in the Movie Maker timeline.

Once your basic sequence is together and the clips are in the right order, you can start to refine it. This is the stage where you do things like trim off that unnecessary footage at the beginning or end of each clip (the handles) or reorder the sequence of clips. This is the real work of the editing process, and there's no one way to do it. You can place all the clips in the sequence you want, then adjust the length of each clip. Or you can edit an individual clip and refine it, then edit and refine another clip, and continue to edit and refine as you go. Along the way you might ask yourself some of the following questions:

- Is the story clear?

- What can I add or take away to make the story clearer?

- Is this section of video necessary?

- If I remove this shot, will it help or hurt the story?

- Is this edit too distracting? What would be better?

- Where does the sequence drag?

Editing is the process of slowly circling in on your story. You will cut, watch what you have, make notes about what to change or fix, then do it all over again. When you're happy with the order and length of your clips, you might want to add transitions and titles, and then music and voice-over to complete your video.

Editing Styles

Understanding the editing process is one thing; developing a personal editing style is another. Editing style refers to the approach you take to string your shots together. There are a few different editing styles vloggers can choose to get started. By familiarizing yourself with different styles, you have some ready-made approaches to draw from when you sit down for your first edit. As you continue to create videos for your vlog, you might decide to mix things up a bit, depending on your subject matter, your intentions, and your mood.

The Single Take

A single take is simply a video that consists of one continuous shot. The camera may be stationery or it may move, but it's still just one shot. This style is used frequently and quite effectively by vloggers (**Figure 5.18**). The major challenge in editing a single take is choosing

Figure 5.18 Jay Dedman's "Looking at Things" from the Momentshowing vlog (www.momentshowing.net/momentshowing/2004/07/videoblog_16_lo.html) is artfully captured in a single take—including the unexpected ending. Pay attention to the pace toward the end, which gives viewers time to absorb the change in setting.

exactly where to start and end the video. If you're editing a video that you planned ahead of time, you've probably rehearsed and worked on the beginning and ending in the shooting process. If, on the other hand, you're editing a video of something you just happened to catch on camera, you'll probably have a number of choices about where to make your edits. If you're not sure where to start or end, ask yourself this question: What is the shortest section necessary to tell the story? While you should aim for brevity when editing footage for your vlog, don't go overboard—it still should be as long as it needs to be to tell your story.

Using B-roll and Cutaways

Let's say you're editing an interview or a shot of someone talking directly to the camera about gourmet coffee. You can use the shot in its entirety if it's the right length and says what you want it to say. But let's say you want to cut out the off-camera questions. Do that and you'll end up with a jump cut, which gives you a splice between two very similar but not identical frames. It's called that because the results can be, well, jumpy. After the cut, the person on camera may appear to "jump" into a different position. One way to visually smooth over a jump cut is to insert a piece of video between the two interview cuts that shows something else that's relevant to the story, perhaps a close-up of a steaming hot cappuccino. This extra footage is referred to as B-roll.

B-roll provides extra visual information that you can use to illustrate what someone is talking about or to provide an additional detail about someone or something. When you're shooting, remember to shoot some B-roll footage so you'll have extra material you can use to cut away from the person speaking to show a different piece of video, while the person's audio continues underneath. These edits are referred to as cutaways (**Figure 5.19**).

Figure 5.19

In Chris Weagel's "The Haberek, Pt.2" from the Human Dog Laboratory vlog (www.human-dog.com/lab/?p=180), B-roll footage was used for cutaways that give us insight into the man being interviewed.

Quick Cuts

Quick cuts let you visually compress the time span of a long sequence by including just enough brief glimpses of the action for an audience to follow the story. Let's say you've filmed a woman walking out of her apartment, waiting for the elevator, riding the elevator down five floors, people entering the elevator along the way, and finally the woman exiting the elevator and the building and walking out to the street. In real time the whole experience took maybe three minutes. If the footage was intended only as a set up for the story that actually took place on the street, those three minutes is probably much too long. Using quick cuts to compress that sequence, you could simply show the apartment door being pulled closed, the elevator door opening in the lobby, and your subject stepping out onto the street. Viewers would still have the facts—that this woman left her apartment and went outside, but they would get them in ten seconds instead of three minutes. This video entitled "Cut" takes the idea of quick cuts to the extreme and transforms what could be a pretty uneventful video of a haircut into a work of art (**Figure 5.20**).

Figure 5.20
Tom Laczny's "Cut," from the Fast Moving Animals vlog (http://fastmovingani-mals.blogspot.com/2006/01/cut.html), condenses a 15-minute haircut into a fast-paced barrage of clips that clock in at less than 60 seconds.

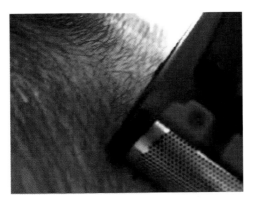

Applying Transitions and Effects

Once cutting is complete, you can consider adding transitions and effects. These are valuable tools in the editing process. Some effects add a certain style or pizzazz to a sequence, while others help you solve problems by polishing a rough edge, changing brightness, or making a two-minute clip play in just a few seconds. Some effects are added to the point between two clips, which is called the edit point. Others are added to an entire clip or group of clips. Let's take a look at applying effects to your sequence.

Transition Effects

The purpose of transitions is exactly what the name suggests: to provide a shift from one shot to another at an edit point. Transitions can give your videos a little extra spunk, a professional look, or a smoothing effect. You can also use them to just add fun to a simple sequence.

There are different types of transitions. The most popular is the *cross dissolve* (**Figure 5.21**). Dissolves blend the end of one image into the beginning of another and are often used to smooth an edit point that's jumpy, jarring, or confusing to viewers. A *fade* transition, which dissolves an image in or out of a blank screen (usually black), can visually imply the passing of time without literally announcing, for example, "one hour later." Other types of transitions include wipes, which use a geometric shape such as a circle to replace one image with another, or some type of push effect that moves an image off the screen revealing the next image in the sequence.

Figure 5.21

In Laczny's video "Heat," long cross dissolves are used to fade one image into another, creating a separate, third image in between. Find it on his vlog at http://fastmovinganimals.blogspot.com/2005/06/heat.html.

Editing applications come with a variety of transitions. You can usually preview a transition before applying it to make sure it creates the effect you want (**Figures 5.22** and **5.23**). Depending on your editing software, you may be able to change the speed of a transition to make it a specific length.

Cross Dissolve

Click the transition for a preview

Speed slider

Timeline

Figure 5.22 iMovie lets you preview a transition while it's selected. To apply a transition, in this case a cross dissolve, drag the transition between any two clips on the timeline (at the bottom of the window).

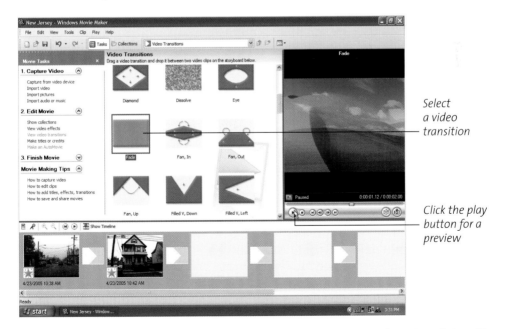

Select a video transition

Click the play button for a preview

Figure 5.23 Windows Movie Maker uses two stock images to give you a quick preview of a transition.

Working with Handles

Remember handles, those extra few seconds before and after the primary action you captured with your clip? Here's where they come in handy. If you don't want a transition to cover important action, add a second onto each end of a clip. Then the transition effect will go from a handle at the end of one clip into the handle at the beginning of the next so the main event will be visible in all its glory.

Motion Effects

Motion effects change the speed of your clips by either slowing down or speeding up the video. Speeding up a clip can condense a long clip into a much faster "time-lapsed" type of shot. Slowing down a piece of video can add emphasis or a dramatic effect. Most editing programs have options for changing a clip's motion or playback time (**Figures 5.24, 5.25**).

Figure 5.24   In Bottom Union's video Dance Dubuffet, http://bottomunion.com/blog/?p=98, a speedy motion effect is used to give a stop motion animation feel to a dancer "sliding" through French artist Dubuffet's public sculpture at Hoge Veluwe National Park, The Netherlands.

Figure 5.25   In 29fragiledays' "Shelter," http://29fragiledays.blogspot.com/2005/04/shelter.html, motion effects are used to slow down and emphasize a single moment that passed too quickly for the eye to fully appreciate at regular speed.

Visual Effects

Visual effects can change the overall look of one or more clips. For example, you can change the style of an image by giving it an "old movie" look complete with scratches and graininess. You can create an artsy look by making it black and white or sepia toned, or give it an action-movie look by shaking it up with an earthquake effect. You can also use a video effect to correct or improve a clip by adjusting the brightness or color of the image (**Figures 5.26, 5.27**).

 Depending on the effect, your computer may need a significant span of time to render it. Rendering is how the computer applies or attaches a video effect to a clip, and some effects take longer than others to render.

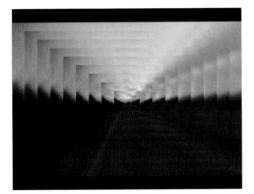

Figure 5.26 In "Blur" (http://www.nearlyenough.com/?p=3), posted on Almost Always Is Nearly Enough, visual effects are used to manipulate the image into layers of blurred landscape, creating a very different video than if the clips were used as they were originally recorded.

Figure 5.27 In the vlog::banal video "The Belt," http:// x.nnon.tv/vlog/2006/01/the_belt.html, footage from Scratch Video is remixed with motion effects to create a Cheshire Cat quality that may not have been intended in the original video.

Effects are fun, but use them in moderation. Try not to go overboard with visual effects, which can overwhelm your audience. In most situations, subtlety is a virtue. If you find that your video truly demands heavily saturated effects, by all means go for it, but be prepared for long render and export times.

Adding Titles

Titles can be used for a variety of purposes in videos. The most obvious application of titles is at the beginning and end to show the name of your video and Web address. It's so easy to copy and post things on the Internet that videos can end up in several places on the Web. Put a Web address on any video you create, and people will be able to trace the origin of your amazing masterpiece and find its creator (**Figure 5.28**). Typically, videobloggers add Web addresses to the final three to five seconds of their videos. Some vloggers create a custom opening sequence with the name of the videoblog, its URL, and the video's title (**Figure 5.29**).

Figure 5.28

Jay Dedman ends each video by showing the Web address of his vlog.

Figure 5.29

Sara Weagel opens every video for Sara's Corner (http://human-dog.com/sara) with a shot of herself under the title of her videoblog.

Titles can also help add context to a story. Who, what, where, when, why? These questions can be easily and artfully answered with the help of titles such as those shown in **Figures 5.30** and **5.31**.

Figures 5.30 and 5.31 In "The Haberek, Pt.1," http://www.human-dog.com/lab/?p=163, Chris Weagel uses simple titles to unobtrusively answer questions about who, where, and when.

Many a vlogger has posted videos with noisy background sound that makes the recorded speech inaudible. Titles can be a great supplement to poor audio recordings as well (**Figure 5.32**).

Figure 5.32 In "Vaccuming," Tim Babarini captured amazing footage of his nephew vacuuming out of boredom. Fortunately for us, Tim used titles to supplement the roaring audio from the vacuum before he posted the video to his vlog, Reality Sandwich (http://realitysandwich.typepad.com/blog/2005/07/vacuuming.html).

Titles can also be used to express the thoughts of a videoblogger. Use them to pose questions or simply add comments along the way (**Figure 5.33**).

Figure 5.33
In "Hey, Let's Go To Harris Ranch!," http://schlomolog .blogspot.com/2005/ 08/hey-lets-go-to- harris-ranch.html, Schlomo of Echoplex Park allows us to peak inside his brain and listen to his innermost rants.

Adding titles to your video is easy. Most applications have a lot of preset title animations to choose from. Just type your text, pick a font and size, give it some color, and add it to a sequence (**Figures 5.34, 5.35**). Depending on the editing program you use, there may be options for animating text as well.

Figure 5.34 To create a title in iMovie, click on the Title option, type your title, choose your options, and drag and drop the title onto a clip in your movie. Titles will appear over video unless you select the Over black box for a black background.

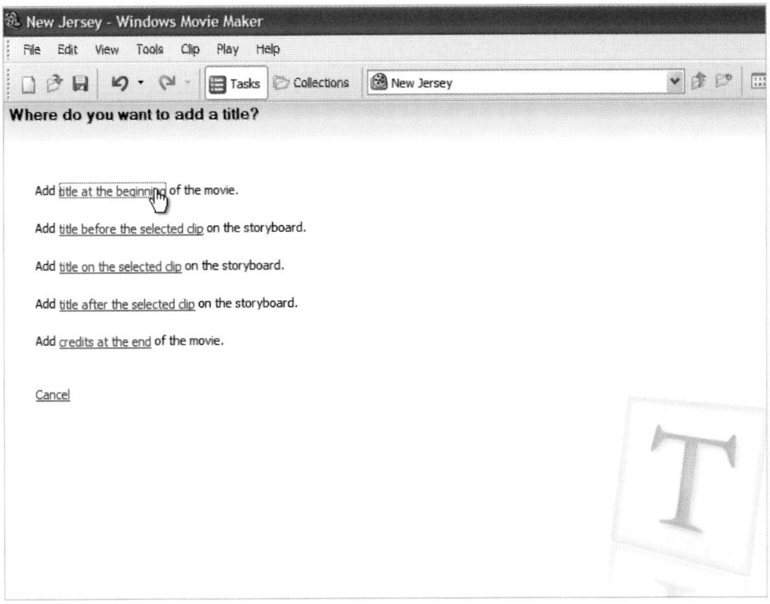

Figure 5.35

There's no dragging and dropping titles with Windows Movie Maker. Instead, you select the location from a menu.

Adding and Mixing Sound

As we've mentioned before, sound is as important to a video as visuals. Music, sound effects, and narration can change the emotional content of your video. It can create the perfect mood, add the right finishing touch, or mix intensity with humor to create a unique perspective. Adding audio files to your project is easy in both iMovie and Movie Maker. You can simply drag your audio files to the bin or in iMovie, use File > Import, or in Movie Maker, File > Import into Collection. Then make sure to switch to the timeline view to work with audio tracks (**Figure 5.36**). After you add individual audio tracks, you'll need to mix them together to create a good, balanced sound (**Figure 5.37**).

Figure 5.36

The Show Timeline button in Movie Maker does just that—shows the timeline.

Figure 5.37
The clock button in iMovie will switch you to timeline view.

Creating Voice-Overs

Sometimes the visuals you choose for your vlog can stand alone. But in some videos, the visuals are not enough. They may need a narration, or *voice-over*, to add editorial comment at specific moments (**Figure 5.38**).

note When adding a voice-over to your vlog, a good rule of thumb is to add extra information with the voice-over instead of simply describing what's happening.

Figure 5.38
In Pouringdown's "Theory: Practice," http://pouringdown.blogspot.com/2006/02/theory-practice.html, a voice-over provides insight into the creator's thoughts about his process for creating videoblogs.

Most editing programs, including iMovie (**Figure 5.39**) and Movie Maker (**Figure 5.40**) have options for recording voice-overs directly into your

Figure 5.39 Because Macs have a built-in mic, you can add a voice-over in iMovie by simply pressing the Record button and talking.

Figure 5.40

You can access the voice-over tool in Windows Movie Maker by clicking the Narrate Timeline button.

sequence. This allows you to record your voice-over while watching the video, rather than having to sync your audio to your video.

Macs and some Windows laptop have built-in microphones. Desktop PCs tend not to have built-in mics but makers often include external mics with their machines. If you have a PC without any mic, or if you have a Mac but you don't like the sound from its built-in mic, consider buying a USB microphone. Logitech (www.logitech.com), for example, offers a desktop microphone for less than $30.

Adding Music

Working with music is another magical element of the editing process. Add the right music to a string of dull images and suddenly they're full of

Figure 5.41

In "Highway of Life," http://dianasallin .blogspot.com/2006/ 02/highway-of-life.html, Diana created a music video by cutting a collage of traveling-down-the-highway images to illustrate her own song.

life. Music can add depth to a scene by underscoring the emotion you've captured in your visuals. It can also add complexity by adding a different mood than what the visuals suggest. You can make music the main event in your video by selecting it first and then editing the visual images to create your own music video (**Figure 5.41**).

If you're a songwriter or simply like putting tracks together using a music-creation program, you can use your own music—and only your own music—however you like (see Chapter 2, "Using Other Material"). Don't forget that Creative Commons has links to free music resources at http://creativecommons.org/audio.

Adding Sound Effects

Sound effects can be a fun element to mix into a soundtrack. But like visual effects, they can be overused and make your video project sound like a Saturday morning cartoon (**Figure 5.42**).

Figure 5.42

iMovie provides a variety of sound effects that you can add to your videos. Simply drag and drop the sound effect from the list to where you want it in your Timeline.

There are plenty of places on the web to find and purchase royalty-free sound effects. However, licenses for the use of these files might not always extend to cover their use in your videos on the web. To be free and clear, we recommend using sites like Ljudo, at http://ljudo.com, where all the sound effects are Creative Commons licensed (**Figure 5.43**).

Figure 5.43

You can search Ljudo for Creative Commons licensed sound effects. These are the results of a search for "laugh."

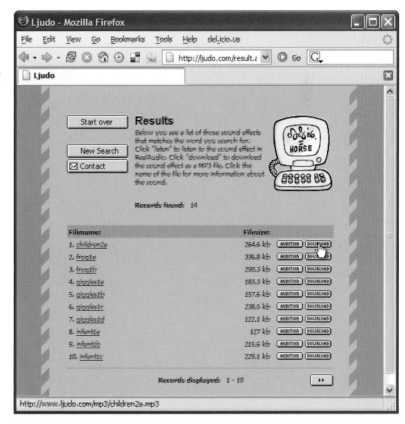

Many videobloggers like to mix sound effects into a soundtrack with a light hand, adding audio flavor so carefully that the audience isn't immediately aware that the soundtrack includes one or more sound effects. **Figure 5.44** offers one example.

Figure 5.44

In Scratch Video's "Collection: QuantumMatter" at www.scratchvideo.tv/scratch/2005/10/collection_quan_1.html, the sound effects are so subtle a viewer can hardly tell what might be effects and what might be part of the video's original sound.

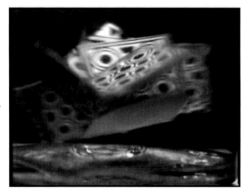

Mixing Audio and Smoothing Cuts

Now that you've added more sound to your video, it's important to make sure that your soundtrack transitions smoothly from one cut to the next, in the same way that your video does. It may be as simple as fading the audio in at the beginning or out at the end. Other times it can be more complex.

The story you are telling helps determine your approach to editing the soundtrack. If your soundtrack includes a conversation, for example, you can smooth an audio transition by making a cut at a natural pause in the conversation. This keeps the audio cut from seeming too abrupt and allows the visuals to keep flowing.

Sometimes cutting from video to a title can sound abrupt and jarring because the video had ambient sound, or *room tone,* and the title was an audio vacuum that had no sound at all. This type of audio jump can be smoothed over by adding a piece of room tone to the title so that the soundtrack is continuous. It's a good idea to record a few seconds of room tone in each location where you shoot video. If you forget, don't panic. After a shoot, there's nearly always a few seconds of footage in which no one speaks that you can use as audio filler if needed.

Pay attention to the visuals in your video and how they interact with any music you've added. For example, be sure to lower your music tracks when people start talking so viewers can actually hear your subject speak. It's fine to keep music underneath an interview, just make sure the sound levels are balanced. The smoother the audio sounds, the smoother the video will seem to your audience.

Polishing the Final Version

After you've added all the bells and whistles to your video, there's one final editing step. Sit back and watch your video straight through. If you're feeling brave, get a friend to watch too and give you feedback. Try to get a feel for the video as a whole. Does it move smoothly? Does the story make sense? Does it feel too long or too short? At first viewing, you may feel the video is complete. But watch it repeatedly, and you may notice a few rough spots that need polishing. You might notice a jump cut that you didn't see before or hear snippets of abrupt sound that need a smoother fade. Take this opportunity to see if every video element fits together and tie up any loose ends.

If you've watched your video 20 times or more over the course of editing and you're not sick of it yet, that's a great sign! Watching sections of your video, cutting or adding effects to it, and then watching it again is the repetitive nature of editing and helps you shape and sculpt your story to perfection.

Get comfortable with editing, because editing is your friend. Every time you edit a piece for your blog, you learn something that prepares you for the next time you shoot. You'll be on the lookout for extra B-roll, ambient sound, and anything else you might have missed the first time around.

masterpiece becomes a skinny 4MB gem that downloads in less than a minute.

The compression software you use to transform a video file lets you fiddle with a variety of factors, including frame size, frame rate, image quality, and audio quality so you can maintain optimal quality overall. For vlogs, you'll reduce the original DV video frame size from 720 by 480 pixels to 320 by 240 pixels, a whopping 78 percent reduction in the number of pixels that make up the image. Other compression techniques are more complex and rely on sophisticated compression/decompression algorithms, called codecs, to perform the necessary audio-video wizardry.

Codecs come in two basic flavors. "Lossless" codecs squeeze files into a smaller space without removing any data. It's a little like stuffing three suits into a small suitcase and then sitting on top of it so you can zip the bag shut. "Lossy" codecs, like the ones you'll use for vlogging, actually reduce the amount of information in a file permanently. That's kind of like fitting your suits into a small bag by snipping off bits of fabric. It may sound drastic, but imagine a skilled tailor trimming fabric from the inside seams; few people would see the difference. Lossy codecs do something similar by removing video and audio information that our eyes and ears don't usually notice and won't miss.

For example, it's hard for the human eye to distinguish between very small differences in color, so video frames can be compressed by averaging out the color in some areas. That means making areas that are similar in color, the same color. Another compression trick saves space by repeating information that's identical from one frame to the next, rather than storing duplicate information for each complete frame.

Compression Tradeoffs

Compression techniques are useful, but they're not foolproof. Some video footage is difficult to compress without a noticeable loss in quality. Flip back to **Figures 4.18** and **4.19** at the end of Chapter 4 to see one example. There are so many areas of small detail that it's not possible to color-average over large areas. Much of the action changes from frame to frame as well, so a codec can't economize by simply repeating redundant information from one frame to the next.

With challenging footage like this, a compression program can usually produce a gorgeous file—if you let it use as much data as it wants. But then you have a file that is much smaller than the original but still too large to post on the Web. To avoid that problem, you can limit the amount of data that a program uses to compress any one frame. But if your limit is too strict and the program doesn't have enough data to do its job, compression artifacts will show up. Viewers will notice blocky chunks of pixels instead of smooth, seamless video. So compression, like so many other aspects of vlogging involves juggling various factors so you can balance the file size you need with the video quality you want.

In Chapter 3 we explained how the various video formats are like containers that hold video and audio information. Any of these formats—.mov, .mpg, .wmv, and .avi—can be compressed with a number of different codecs, each with its own advantages and disadvantages. For now, we recommend that vloggers use the MPEG-4 codec for compression. We find it does the best job of compressing files efficiently while maintaining video quality.

There are several different versions of MPEG-4 codecs out there, including plain-vanilla MPEG-4, H.264, 3ivx, and the version Microsoft created for Windows Media files. The versions you'll use for vlogging don't produce the ultimate in either video quality or file size, but they are compatible with older computers and Web browser plug-ins, and best of all, exist within the software already on your computer. So keep reading!

iMovie Compression (Mac)

There are a number of small steps to follow in order to get a well-compressed video out of iMovie. We've organized them into two parts, "Exporting to QuickTime" and "Entering Compression Settings." That's the bad news. The good news is that once you follow the process described in both sections, iMovie will remember the compression

File	Edit	View	Markers

New...   ⌘N
Open...   ⌘O
Open Recent   ▶

Make a Magic iMovie...

Close Window   ⌘W
Save Project   ⌘S
Save Project As...
Revert to Saved...

Import...   ⇧⌘I
Export...   ⇧⌘E
Burn Project to Disc...

Show Info...   ⌘I
Save Frame...   ⌘F

Show Trash...   ⇧⌘T
Empty Trash...   ⇧⌘⌫

Figure 6.1 In iMovie, choose File >
Export.

settings (unless you change them), so in the future,
you'll only need to do the export steps. There's more
good news: The QuickTime .mov file you create for the
Web will also be compatible with iPods!

Part 1: Exporting to QuickTime

To get your movie out of the editing application and
start the compression process in QuickTime, you will
access iMovie's Export command, choose QuickTime
as the export option, and give your movie a name.
Follow the steps in **Figures 6.1** through **6.5** to get
going.

Because this is the first time you've compressed a
project with QuickTime, you need to click the Options
button to the right of the Export Menu and follow the
steps in Part 2 to enter your compression settings. In the
future, you can just click Save at this point and you'll
be done.

Figure 6.2

Ignore the many
tempting options in
the "Compress Movie
For" pop-up menu
(such as Web and Web
Streaming). Choose
Expert Settings instead
so you can customize
your options. Then click
Share.

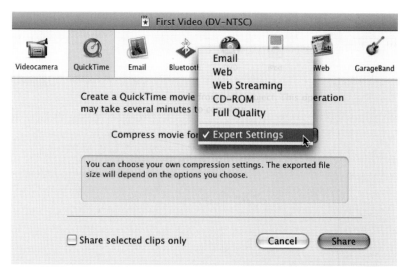

Figure 6.3

Even though it now looks as if iMovie is ready to compress, wait a few seconds for the Save Exported File As dialog box to appear.

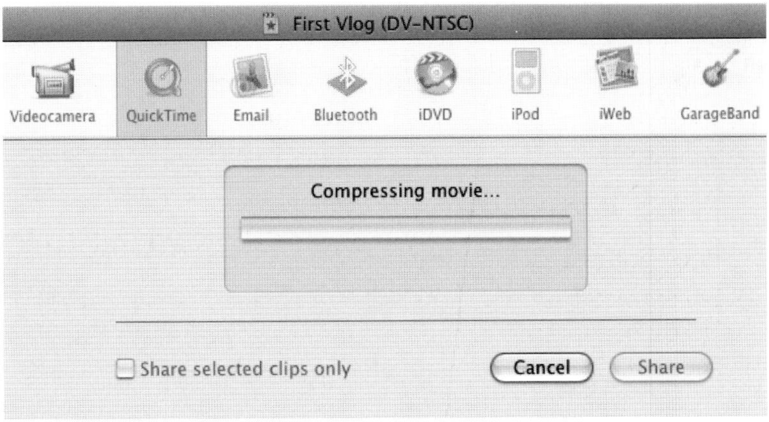

Figure 6.4

Give your file a name and select your project folder as its destination. *But don't click Save yet.*

Figure 6.5

Click the Export pop-up menu at the bottom of the window and choose Movie to QuickTime Movie. No, don't click Save yet!

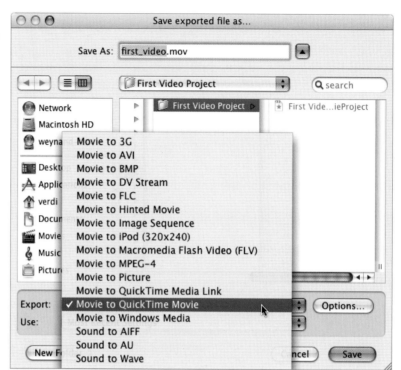

Part 2: Entering Compression Settings

Now you'll select the codec and the specific settings needed to compress your movie. First, in the Save Exported File As dialog, click the Options button next to the Export pop-up menu to bring up the Movie Settings dialog. This is where you enter all of the compression settings. Now follow the steps described in **Figures 6.6** to **6.12** to complete the process.

note If you ever export a video to QuickTime for a non-vlog project and change the settings you've just entered, you'll need to repeat both parts of the process above and reenter those compression settings to create a QuickTime movie for your videoblog and iPods.

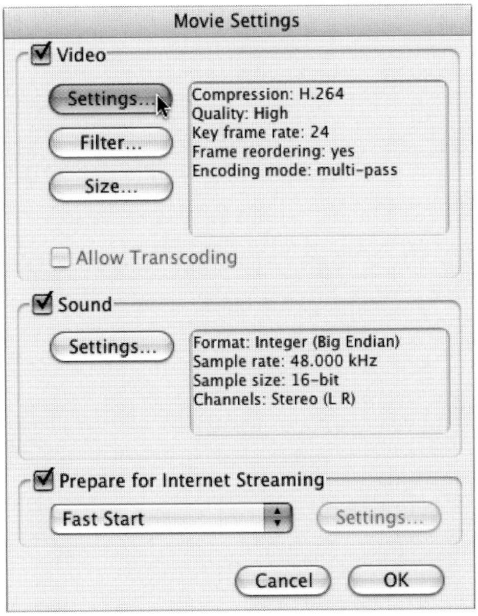

Figure 6.6
Click the Settings button in the Video section.

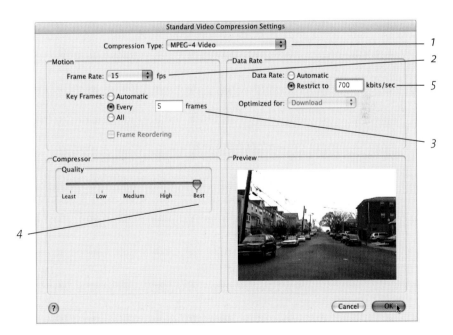

Figure 6.7 Change the Compression Type to MPEG-4 Video and then configure the frame rate, key frame rate, image quality, and data rate as shown here. Click OK when you're done.

Figure 6.8

Back in the Video section of the Movie Settings window, click Size. The Export Size Settings dialog opens. Click the Use Custom Size option and enter 320 as the width and 240 as the height. Then click OK.

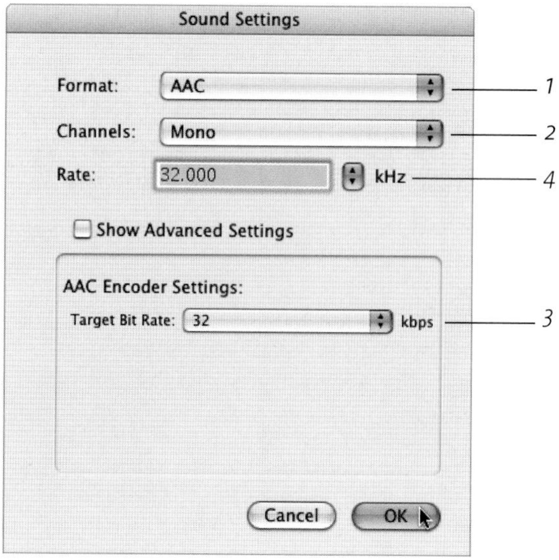

Export Size Settings

○ Use current size
◉ Use custom size

Width: 320

Height: 240

Cancel   OK

Figure 6.9

In the Sound section of the Movie Settings window, click Settings. In the Sound Settings dialog, choose AAC from the Format pop-up menu and then choose the Channel, bitrate, and kilohertz settings shown here. Click OK when you're done.

Sound Settings

Format: AAC —————— 1

Channels: Mono —————— 2

Rate: 32.000   kHz —————— 4

☐ Show Advanced Settings

AAC Encoder Settings:

Target Bit Rate: 32   kbps —————— 3

Cancel   OK

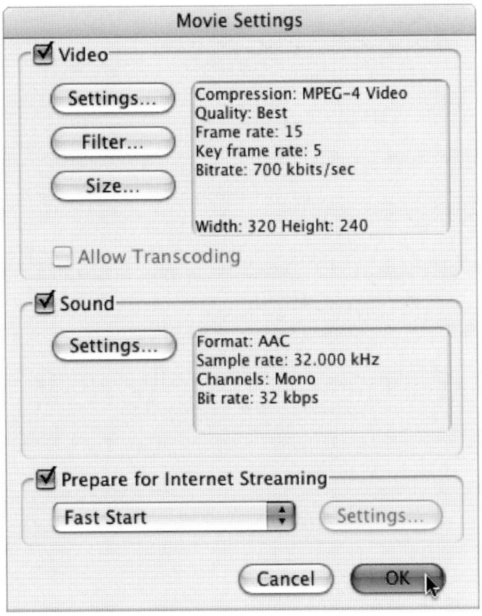

Figure 6.10

Your Movie Settings should look like this. Make sure that Fast Start is selected under the Prepare for Internet Streaming section (it should be selected by default), then click OK.

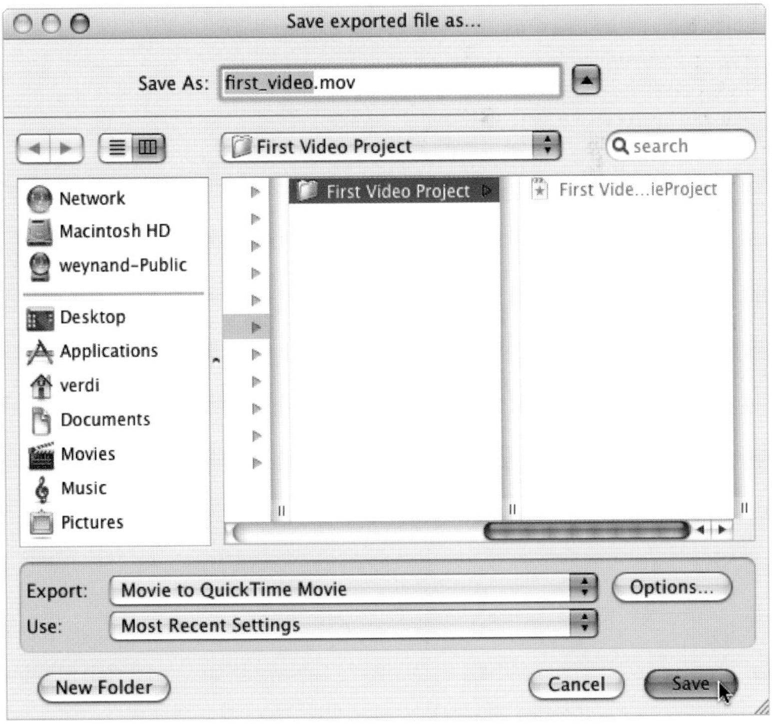

Movie Settings

☑ Video

Settings...
Filter...
Size...

Compression: MPEG-4 Video
Quality: Best
Frame rate: 15
Key frame rate: 5
Bitrate: 700 kbits/sec

Width: 320 Height: 240

☐ Allow Transcoding

☑ Sound

Settings...

Format: AAC
Sample rate: 32.000 kHz
Channels: Mono
Bit rate: 32 kbps

☑ Prepare for Internet Streaming

Fast Start   Settings...

Cancel   OK

Figure 6.11

In the Save Exported File As window, click Save.

Save exported file as...

Save As: first_video.mov

First Video Project

Q search

Network
Macintosh HD
weynand–Public

Desktop
Applications
verdi
Documents
Movies
Music
Pictures

First Video Project ▷   First Vide…ieProject

Export: Movie to QuickTime Movie   Options...
Use: Most Recent Settings

New Folder   Cancel   Save

Figure 6.12

Your video will start to compress and be saved in your video project folder.

Beware the "Movie to iPod" Option

You may have noticed the "Movie to iPod" option when you were compressing your video in iMovie. Have we been holding out on you? Not hardly. We'd love to recommend that option because it uses the H.264 codec, which produces video with amazing quality. But at the time of this writing we've noticed some unresolved issues.

If you use this option to compress DV video, the resulting file is 320 by 213 pixels instead of 320 by 240 pixels, which has the effect of squishing everything in your video vertically so people look short and fat. Another problem is that the compressed video file has an .m4v extension, which currently causes some problems with certain Web servers and browsers. Additionally, the H.264 codec is compatible only with version 7 of the QuickTime player, and some older computers have difficulty playing video compressed with H.264.

For all those reasons we recommend you stick with iMovie's regular MPEG-4 codec when compressing video for iPod fans. That way, the compressed file will be compatible with both versions 6 and 7 of the QuickTime player, and it will playback well on older computers. And the people in your video will look like themselves!

Windows Movie Maker Compression

When you compress your video in Windows Movie Maker, you'll be making a .wmv (Windows Media) file. There's a nice wizard that walks you through the process and includes a good compression preset so

you don't have to enter everything by hand. See what we mean by
following the steps in **Figures 6.13** to **6.20.**

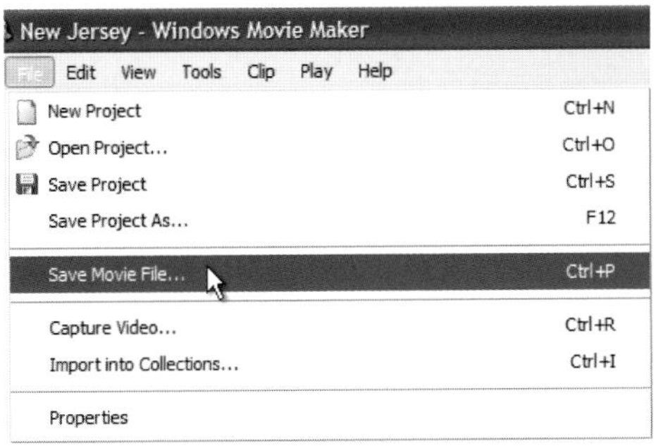

Figure 6.13

With your project open
in Movie Maker, choose
File > Save Movie File,
or press the keyboard
shortcut, Ctrl + P.

Figure 6.14

Choose My Computer
as the place where you
want to save your
movie file.

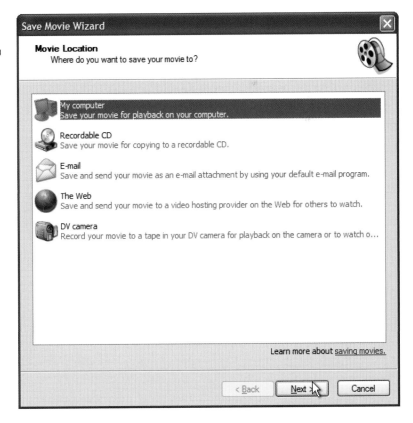

Figure 6.15
Give your file a name and click Browse.

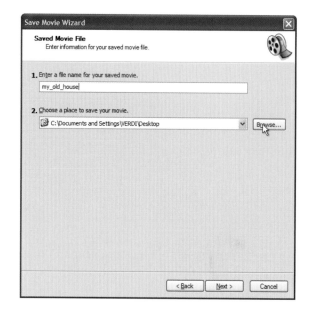

Figure 6.16
Find and select your video project folder as the destination for your compressed movie file. Click OK, and when the previous dialog reappears, click Next.

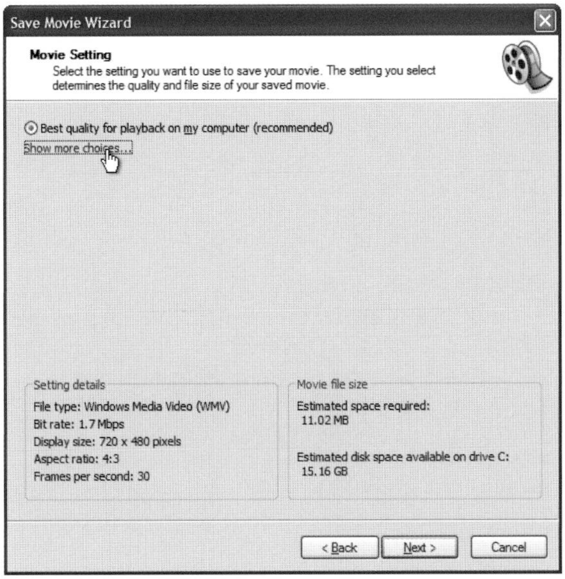

Figure 6.17 Back in the Movie Setting dialog, click Show More Choices.

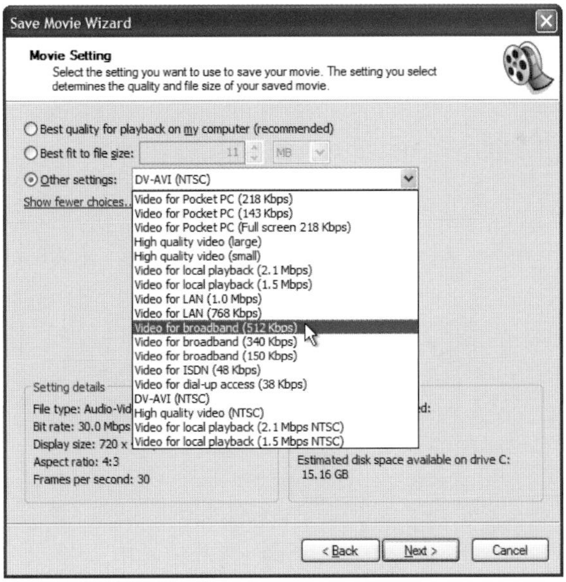

Figure 6.18 Select Other Settings, choose Video For Broadband (512kbps) from the pop-up menu, and click Next.

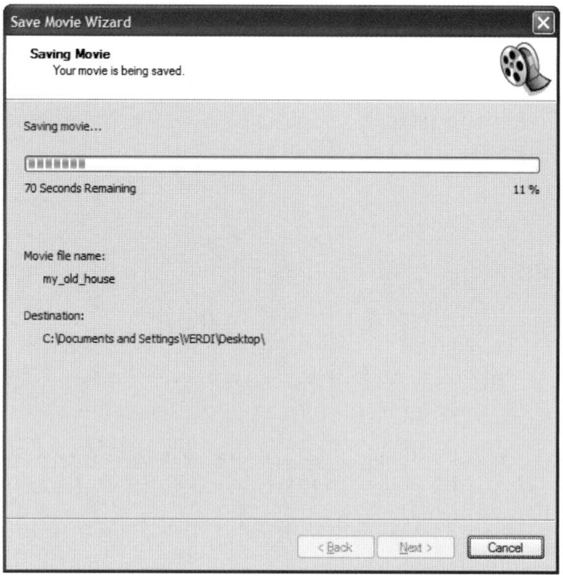

Figure 6.19 Movie Maker will now begin compressing your video. Compression time depends on the speed of your computer, but it's usually about equal to the length of your video. So a two-minute video usually takes about two minutes to compress.

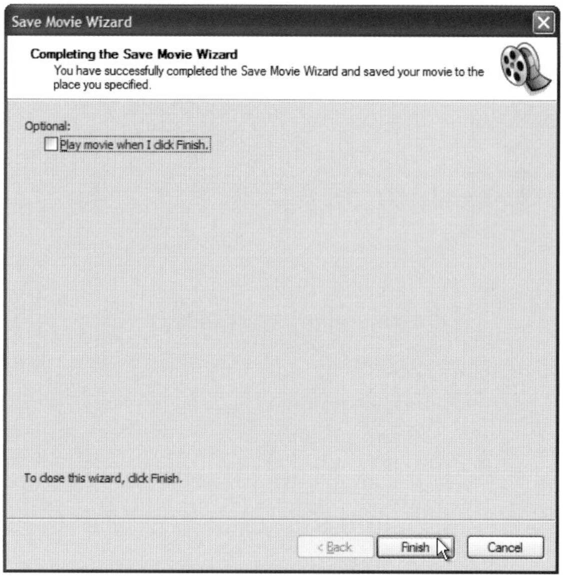

Figure 6.20 After the Save Movie Wizard tells you compression is completed, click Finish.

Whether you use a PC or a Mac, remember to keep all the files on a single video project in one folder. That will make it easier to back up your project and later remove it from your hard drive to make room for new projects.

iPod Compatibility for Windows

As we've noted, the iPod is very picky about what it plays, namely QuickTime movies only and only certain ones at that. (iPod movies must have audio compressed with the AAC Audio codec, for example.) This means .wmv files definitely won't work. It's a two-part process to make your movie compatible with iPods, and it requires a copy of QuickTime 7 Pro. (You can download it for $29.99 at www.apple.com/quicktime/download/win.html.)

Before you can work with your movie in QuickTime Pro, you'll need to save the file in a format that QuickTime can open. This is simple, and the first three steps will be familiar.

Part 1: Exporting a DV-AVI file

Once again you're going to open your video project in Windows Movie Maker, and save your video to your computer but this time you'll save it in a different format. Start by choosing File > Save Movie File, and selecting My Computer as the place where you want to save your movie file. Then name your file and click Browse to locate and select your video project folder.

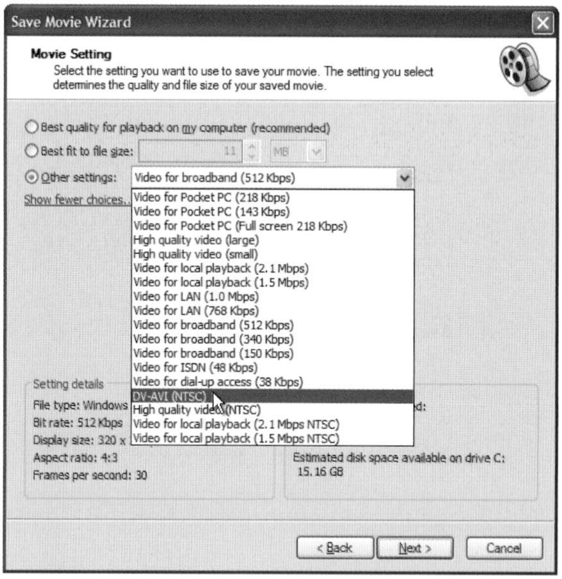

Figure 6.21

When you get to the Movie Setting dialog box, click Select Other Settings and choose DV-AVI (NTSC) from the pop-up menu. Then click Next. Movie Maker will save your movie as a full resolution DV file.

Part 2: Compressing with QuickTime Pro

Now that you have a full-resolution DV file, you can use QuickTime Pro to compress it for iPods by following the steps in **Figures 6.22** through **6.29**.

 note If you ever export a video for another reason and change these settings, you'll need to go through the process again and re-enter these compression settings to create iPod-compatible files.

Figure 6.22
Open the file you just created and choose File > Export.

Figure 6.23
Name the file a name and select Movie to QuickTime Movie from the Export pop-up menu. Then click the Options button to configure everything. QuickTime Pro will save all your settings, so in the future you can just click Save to compress your video.

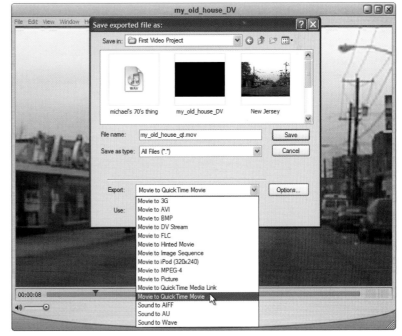

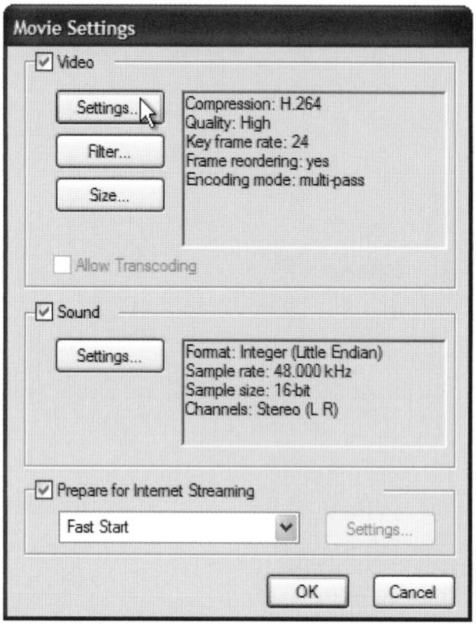

Figure 6.24

Click the Options button again to bring up the Movie Settings dialog box, then click Settings under the Video section.

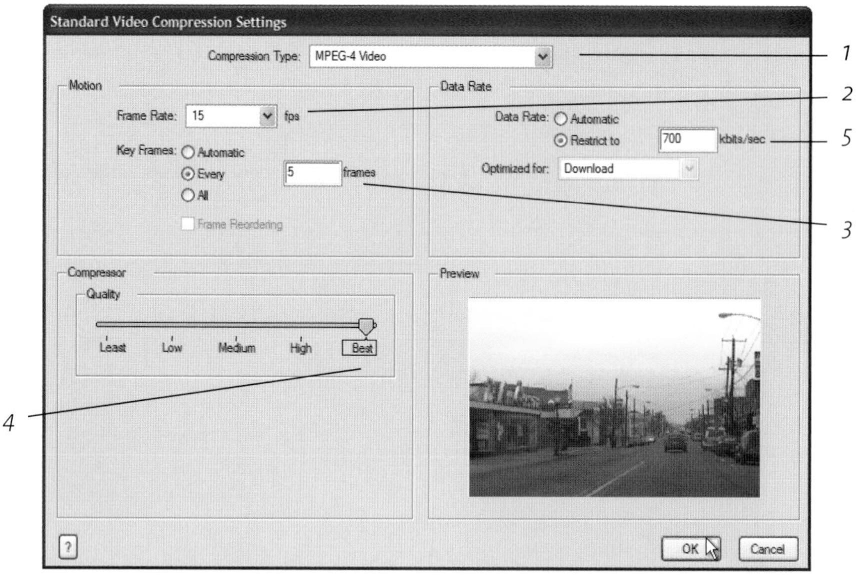

Figure 6.25 Configure the video settings as shown: first choose MPEG-4 Video compression, 15 fps, keyframes every 5 frames, and best quality compression. Finally, set the data rate to 700 kbits per second. Now click OK.

Figure 6.26

Click OK to return to Movie Settings, then click Size to set a custom size of 320 pixels wide and 240 pixels high. Click OK.

Figure 6.27

Now click the Settings button under the Audio section. Then configure the audio settings as shown: first AAC format, Mono for channels, and a target bit rate of 32 kbps. Finally, set the kHz to 32,000, and click OK.

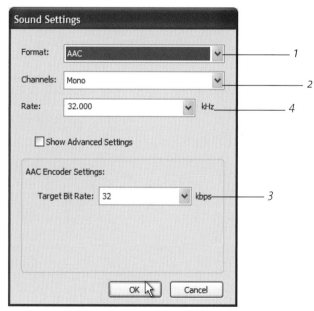

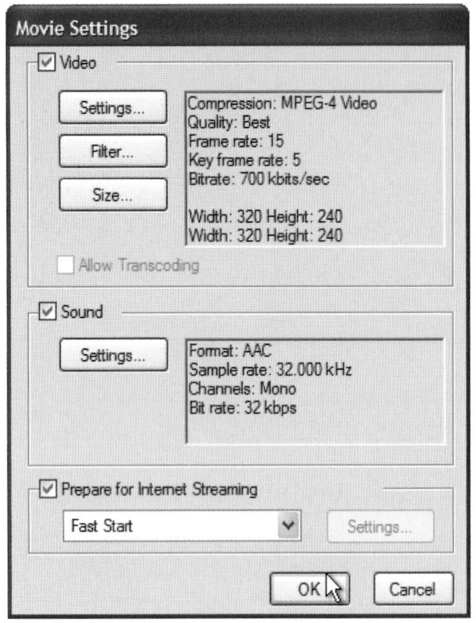

Figure 6.28

Your Movie Settings should look like this. Make sure that Fast Start is selected under the Prepare for Internet Streaming section (it should the default), then click OK.

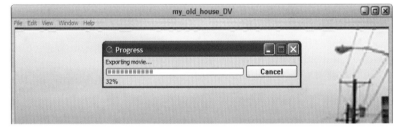

Figure 6.29

Click Save, and your video will start compressing. Depending on the speed of your computer, this usually takes about twice as long as your video. So a two-minute video should take about four minutes to compress.

Creating a Screenshot

So now your video is ready to post, but you will need an image to represent it so your viewers will know what to expect. Many vloggers show a frame from each video they post so it displays within the video player (**Figure 6.30**). It's an instant way to let people know a Web site

Figure 6.30

Using a screenshot of the QuickTime or Windows Media Player window makes it obvious to your viewers that they're about to click on a link to a video file, not a still photograph.

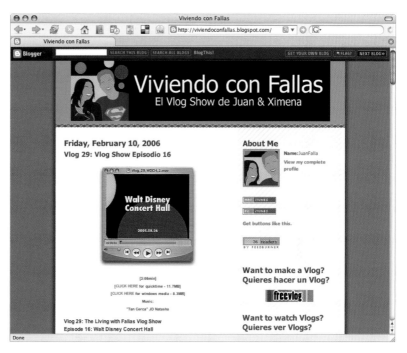

contains videos rather than photographs. You, too, can make your vlog a recognizable video-viewing hotspot. In this section we'll show you how to create a screenshot of your video. In the next chapter you will learn how to actually post your video to the Web and how to post the image you're about to create as a link your video. Then when someone clicks on the image, your video will begin to play automatically. Follow the steps in **Figures 6.31** through **6.38**.

Capturing Screenshots on a PC

On a PC, you have the ability to change how the Windows Media Player window looks by making changes in Skin Mode.

Figure 6.31

Open your compressed .wmv file. If your Windows Media Player isn't in Skin Mode, choose View > Skin Mode. This will make the player small, and the resulting image will fit on your vlog.

Figure 6.32 To get the video image to show up in the screenshot, you need to temporarily change a setting in Windows Media Player. Choose Tools > Options.

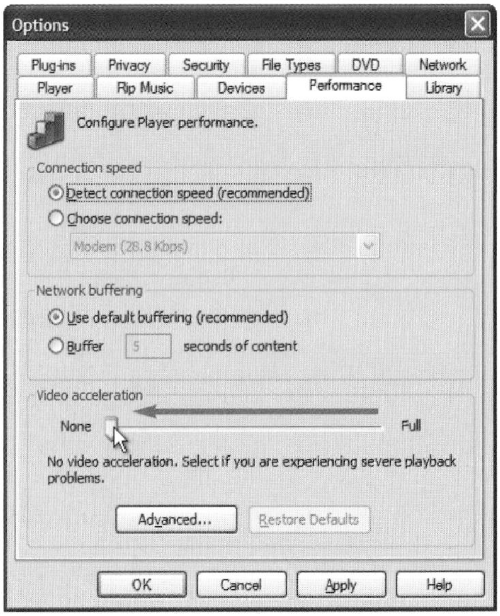

Figure 6.33 Select the Performance tab and change Video Acceleration from Full to None. (After taking the screenshot, you can reset it back to Full if you wish.)

Figure 6.34 Now play your video and pause it on a frame that best represents the video. When you've got the frame you want, press Alt + PrintScreen (or PrtSc, depending on your keyboard) to take a picture of the Media Player window copy it to the clipboard.

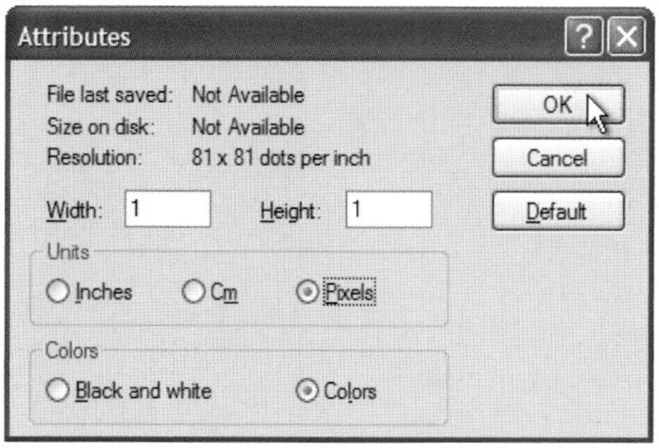

Figure 6.35 Next, open the Paint program by going to Start > All Programs > Accessories. Size the document so that it's smaller than the image that you'll paste into it. If not, you'll end up with a bunch of white space to one side of the image. Now choose Image > Attributes and change the width and height of the document to 1 pixel each.

Figure 6.36
Choose Edit > Paste and your picture will appear in Paint.

Figure 6.37

Now choose File > Save and name your image. Be sure to choose JPEG from the Save As pop-up menu, then click Save.

Figure 6.38

Your finished JPEG should look like this. Congratulations, it's now ready for uploading to the Web, which we cover in the next chapter.

Capturing Screenshots on a Mac

To get a screenshot of your entire QuickTime movie window, follow the steps below.

When you finish, it will be ready for uploading to the Web, which we cover in the next chapter.

Figure 6.39
Open your compressed QuickTime .mov file, and press Cmd+Shift+4. Rather than using the cross-hairs to select a portion of the screen, press the Space bar to take a picture of the entire window. When the camera icon appears, position it over the QuickTime window and click the mouse button.

Figure 6.40
The screenshot will appear on your desktop as Picture 1 in PNG format. Double-click this file to open it in the Preview application (Figure 6.41).

Figure 6.41

Here's a screen capture of your video in the QuickTime player. Looks so real, you've tempted to click the play button—but not yet!

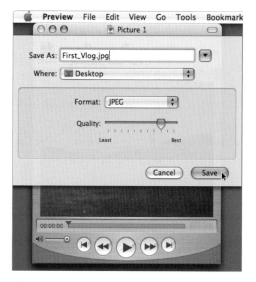

Figure 6.42 In Preview, choose File > Save As, rename your picture, choose JPEG under the format menu, and click Save.

Figure 6.43 The finished screen shot for your vlog. Congratulations! Your finished JPEG should look like this.

Vlog

7

This is the moment you've been working toward, when you actually get to build your videoblog! To create your vlog, you will need to create accounts with several different sites. One is where your vlog page can be found, so the world can watch the videos you create. The other is where you'll actually keep your videos. The latter is, in essence, a media library that not only lets you check out other people's work but also lets you add your own material to its shelves.

After that, you'll link your movie to your vlog site and *voilà*, people can finally view your masterpiece.

So, How's a Vlog Different from a Web site?

Don't be surprised if after you start videoblogging friends and family ask you how a video-blog differs from a normal Web site that features video.

The biggest benefit of a blog, compared to a regular Web site, is that blogging software automatically generates an RSS feed.

The ability to send regular updates to your subscribers is, by itself, reason enough to vlog. Add to that the fact that vlogs are easy to build and easy to maintain—hey, what more do they need to be convinced?

Naming Your Vlog

When you set up a vlog, you need to decide two things: the name or title of your vlog, which will appear at the top of the vlog page, and its URL. Before you make any decisions, though, keep in mind two things:

- Your vlog's title and its Web address don't have to be the same.

- It's easy to change the title of a vlog, but it's hard to change its URL.

Picking one is harder than it sounds. You might easily come up with half a dozen URLs but the question is whether they're available. You might be surprised by how many names are already taken—including weird ones. So it's best to make a list of several alternatives and have them ready if you need them. That way, if bestvideoblogever is unavailable, you can try bestvlog or thebestvideoblog.

We happen to use Blogger, so if we succeeded in choosing bestvideoblogever before others got it, the URL would be this: http://bestvideoblogever.blogspot.com.

Different blogging apps handle names differently, but you get the concept.

It's easy to change the title whenever you feel like it. Changing the URL, however, won't be nearly as easy. You'll have to establish another blog at a new address and then notify all your friends and fans about the move. In the process, you may lose some visitors because search engines will be linking to your old URL, not your new one, at least for a while. And if you care about your old archives, you'll need to copy them from the old site to add them to the new site. For all these reasons, choose a URL carefully.

Creating a Blog Account

In the steps below we show you how to create a blog using Firefox and Blogger, which is run by Google. There are other choices (see "Free Blogging Sites"), but we love Blogger because it's free, easy, ad-free, and archived.

To get started, open your browser and go to http://blogger.com. Click the big orange arrow that says, "Create Your Blog Now" (**Figure 7.1**). Now follow the steps described in **Figures 7.2** to **7.10**.

Figure 7.1
It's fast and easy to create a blog with Blogger.

Free Blogging Sites

There are many free blogging services available, and millions of people blog on LiveJournal, WordPress.com, MySpace, or Xanga. All of these services work well for vloggers, and you create a vlog with them in the same way you do with Blogger. You open a blog account, upload your video at Ourmedia, post the screenshot your made on your blog, and link it to your video.

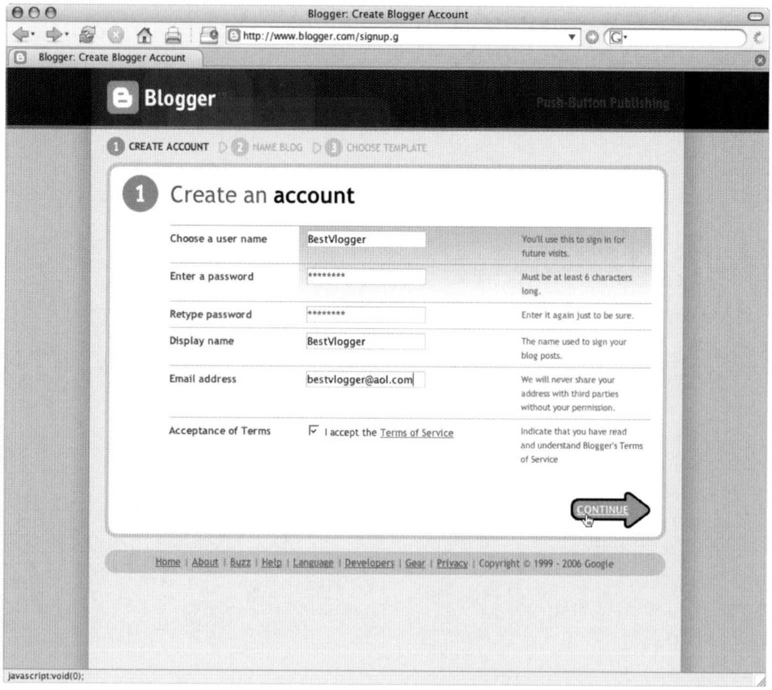

Figure 7.2

When the Create an Account page appears, type in a user name, password (something you'll remember), display name (it can be the same as your user name), and your email address. Be sure to read the Terms of Service before you click the box to accept them. Now click the big orange arrow to continue.

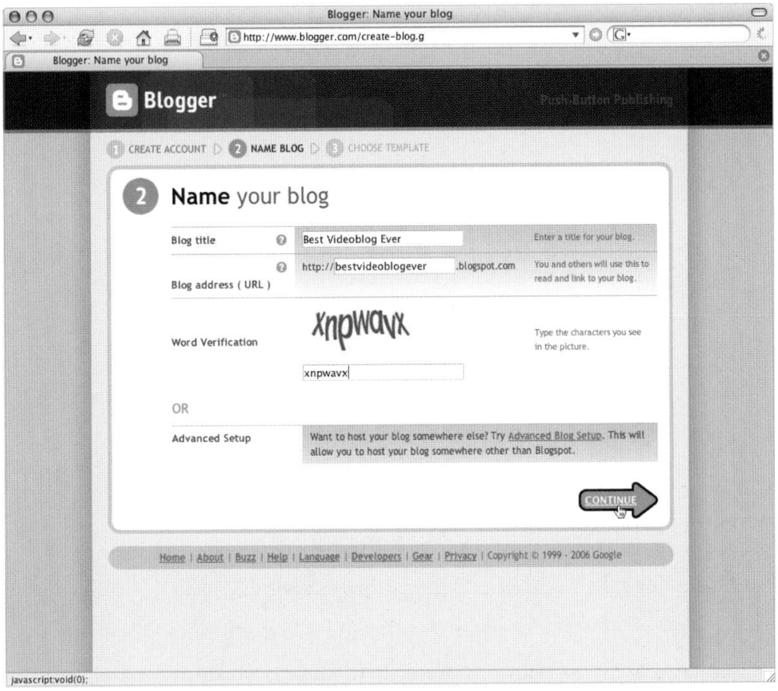

Figure 7.3

It's time for the big moment—naming your blog and choosing its Web address. Enter a blog title and a blog address. Remember, the title can be changed easily but not the URL, so type in an address you plan to keep. Enter the word Blogger shows you and then click the big orange arrow.

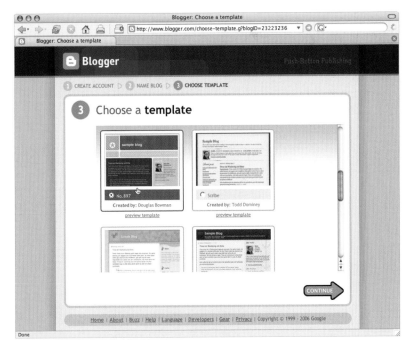

Figure 7.4

Blogger has 12 preset templates, each offering a different look for your blog. You can preview each template by clicking the Preview Template link below its picture. To choose a look for your blog, click a template you like. (You can switch to a different template at any time.) Then click the orange arrow.

Figure 7.5

First you'll get a message screen that says Blogger is creating your blog.

Figure 7.6

Then you'll get a message screen that says your blog has been created. Congratulations! Click the orange Start Posting arrow to create your first blog posting.

Figure 7.7

Your blog won't actually exist on the Web until you publish your first entry. The first post can be basic, like the one we've created here, or it can be a short introduction to your vlog. What it says isn't as important as what it does, which is make your blog real. Give your post a title in the title field, then add some text in the large text field. Click the orange Publish Post button to add this entry to your blog.

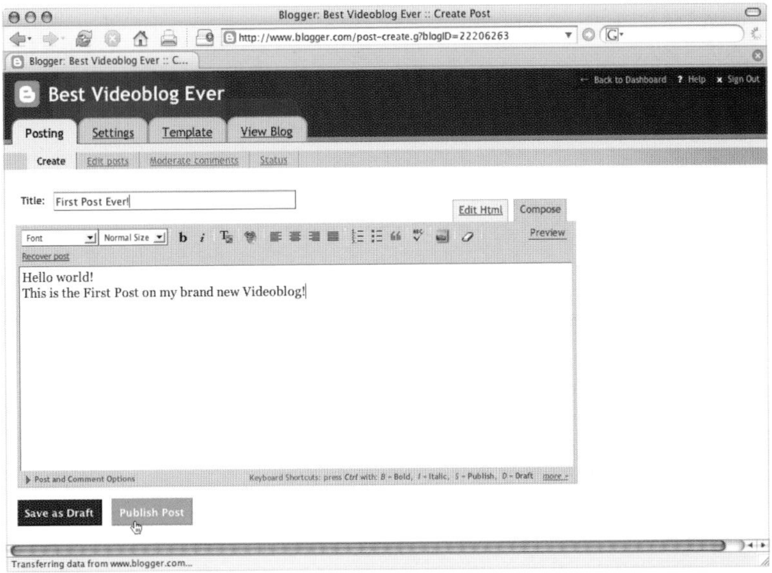

Figure 7.8

Now you'll get a message screen that says publishing is in progress, which shouldn't take long.

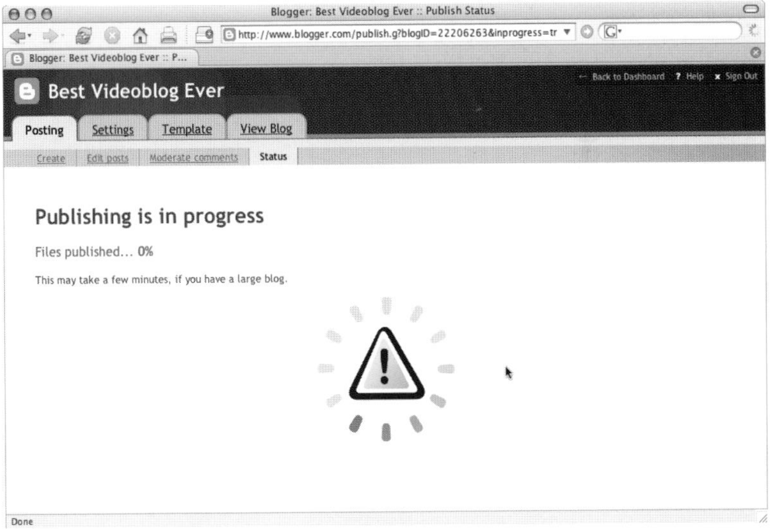

Figure 7.9

Blogger will tell you when your post has been published. Click the View Blog link to see the results.

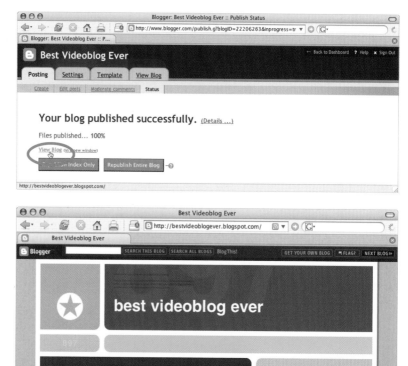

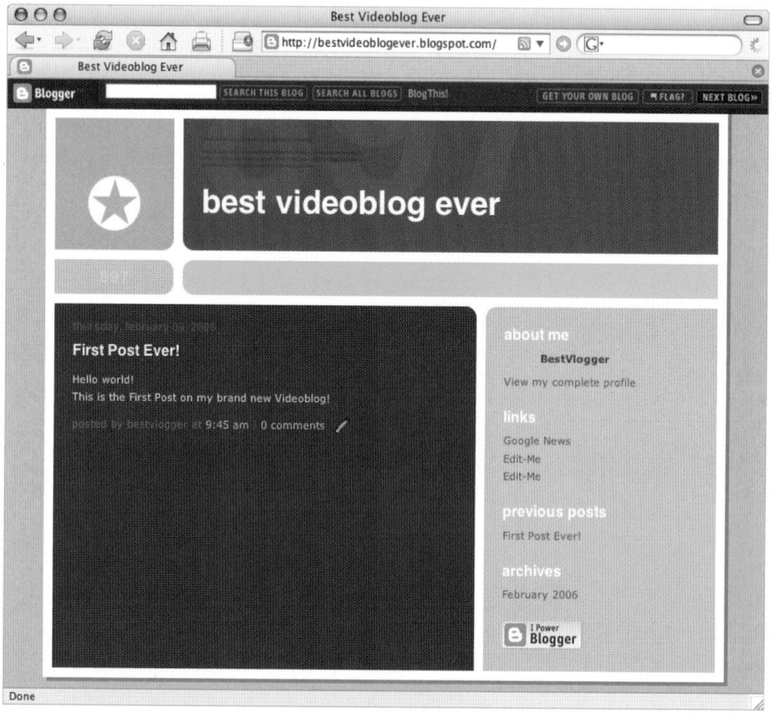

Figure 7.10

Ta-dah! Your blog is in place and you're ready to attach your video.

Stylish Blogger Templates

Want a look that's not offered in Blogger's template selection? Check out http://blogger-templates.blogspot.com or search on *blogger templates* for more choices. After you find a design you like, copy its code (which is provided on template sites), go into your Blogger Dashboard, click the Template tab, and paste the code into the text field below.

Finding a Video Host

Now you've created a blog, but you still need to find a video host. As we explained earlier, your video will be hosted, or stored, by a different service than your blog. Then your video will be linked to your blog to make it a videoblog. Until recently, storing videos on the Internet was a pretty expensive proposition. That's because even in their compressed form, video files take up a lot of bandwidth—way more than photos and text. In fact, entire Web sites often take up less space than a single video. And Web servers, which host Web pages and have limited bandwidth—they can only handle so much data per second. But as Web server prices have gone down, free video hosting services have begun to appear.

One prime example of free media hosting is provided by the partnership of The Internet Archive (http://archive.org), and Ourmedia (http://ourmedia.org). The mission of The Internet Archive, aka The Archive, is to document all human knowledge in one place, kind of like a huge, online library or enormous multimedia encyclopedia (say that 10 times fast). The site's tagline is "Universal access to human knowledge," and on The Archive you'll find archives of audio, video, text, and live music (Grateful Dead fans, this is your heaven).

Ourmedia, which calls itself "the Global Home for Grassroots Media," is a nonprofit online community "dedicated to spreading grassroots creativity" in all its digital forms. Together they offer videobloggers the amazing opportunity to post media files for free, forever (at least, if all goes according to plan)—no gimmicks, no joke. Basically, The Archive has agreed to host media files posted by Ourmedia members. If The Archive is like a vast online library system, Ourmedia is like a local branch library that makes uploading and storing media easy.

Opening an Archive Account

To upload your videos to The Archive via Ourmedia, you need to set up an account and get a virtual library card. It's a quick, two-step process.

First, open your browser and go to http://archive.org to open an account at The Archive. Click the tiny Join Us link in the upper right corner of the site (**Figure 7.11**).

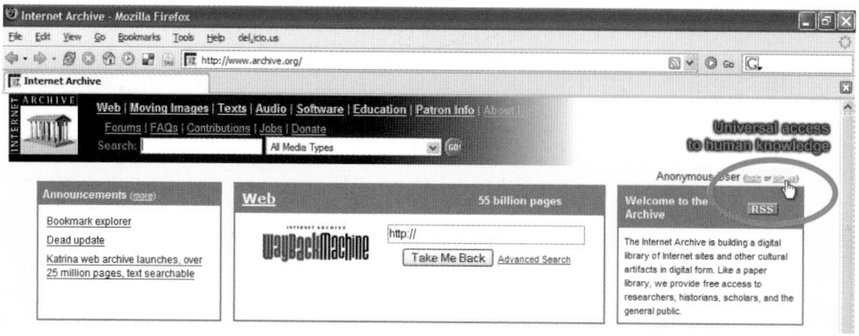

Figure 7.11

The Archive just may be the coolest multimedia library on the planet.

Second, fill in the fields with your email address, a password, and a Screen name. Click Get Library Card (**Figure 7.12**).

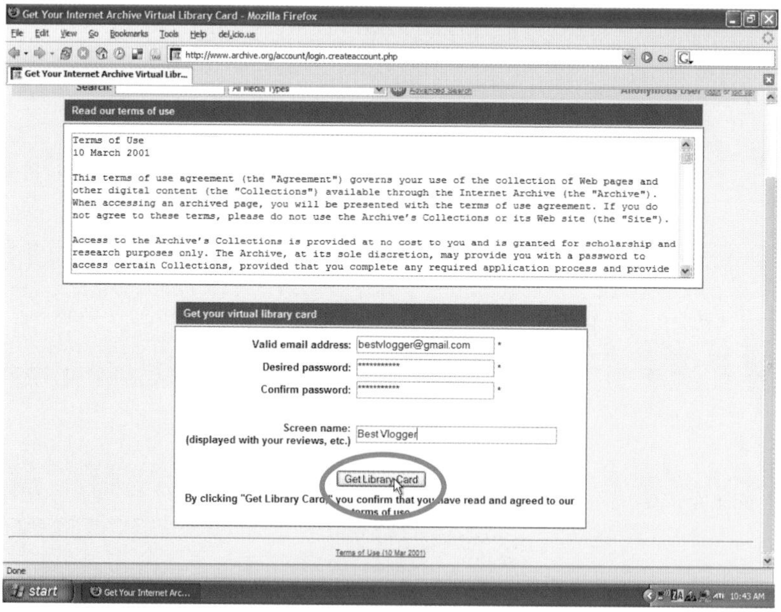

Figure 7.12

Getting your virtual library card is quick and easy.

You will see a quick Congratulations screen and then you'll be redirected to the home page. It's that simple.

Uploading Your Video

With your Archive account set up, you'll log on to the Ourmedia site and upload your media file. Then we'll show you how to link your video to your blog so people can view it. Don't let the number of steps fool you. The entire process is easy, and you'll quickly become an expert.

First, go to the Ourmedia homepage at http://ourmedia.org. Click the Log in button in the upper right corner of the page (**Figure 7.13**), which will take you to the "my page" section of the site. You'll need to sign in to the service by using your password and user ID from The Archive—which, oddly enough, is your email address and *not* your screen name. Now follow the directions in **Figures 7.14** to **7.19** to upload your video.

Figure 7.13
Setting up a free account is quick and easy.

Figure 7.14
Find My Controls in the left column of the page, and click the Publish My Media link.

Figure 7.15

In the Publish My Media section, click the Video icon.

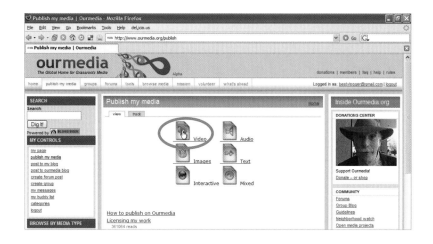

Figure 7.16

In the Submit Video area, fill in all required fields (those with red asterisks). Be sure that the Description of work is at least five words long. This description will not appear on your blog, but the words you enter could be used as keywords to search through the archive for your video.

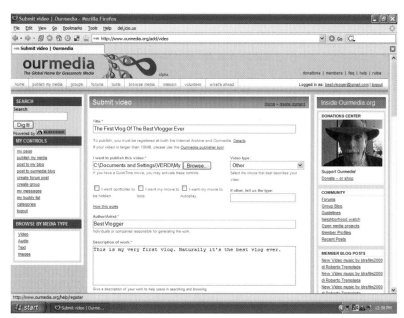

Figure 7.17

Under the Basic Details section is the Creative Commons license menu. The most common license used by videobloggers is Attribution Non-commercial Share Alike (by-nc-sa), but you can decide which options best suit your video.

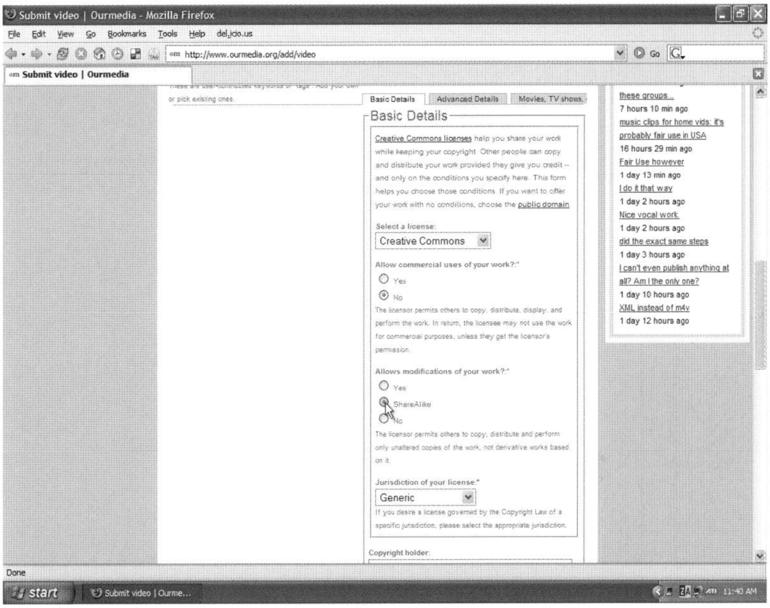

Figure 7.18

Click Submit to upload your video. Be patient, this can take a little while depending on your connection and file size. While your video uploads, it will look as if nothing is happening.

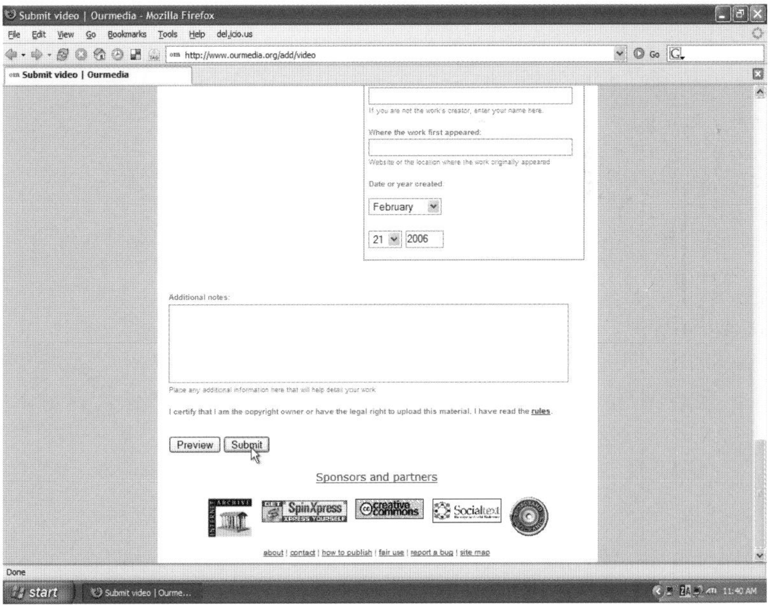

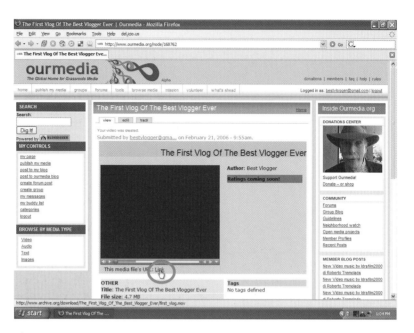

Figure 7.19   When your video has been uploaded, a new page with your media will appear. You'll need to copy the video file address or URL for linking on your blog. Underneath the video itself, there is a link that says "This media file's URL: Link." Right +click (or Ctrl + click, if you're on a Mac) and select Copy Link Location. Keep this copied while you create a post and paste it into your blog.

note   Make sure you don't accidentally click the video's URL and copy the URL in the address bar. This is a temporary URL that will eventually stop working.

Back to Blogger for More Posting

Great work! You've uploaded your video and copied the URL. Now, you need to go back to your blog to create a new post specifically for your video. Remember the screenshot you took in the previous chapter? Here's where that comes in. If you've logged out of Blogger, log back in and click the New Post button in your Blogger Dashboard (**Figure 7.20**), then follow the steps shown in **Figures 7.21** to **7.26**.

Figure 7.20

If necessary, log back in to Blogger.com and click the New Post button in your Blogger Dashboard.

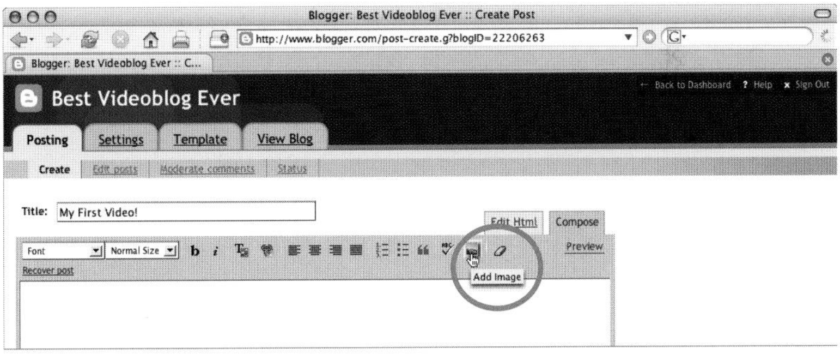

Figure 7.21

Type a title for your videoblog post in the Title field. Click the Add Image button to upload your screenshot to your blog post.

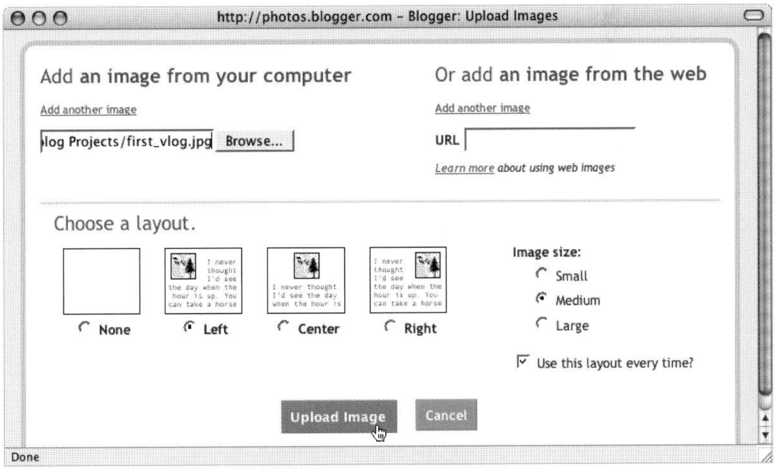

Figure 7.22

Click the Browse button under Add another image from your computer section on the right side of the window. Look in your Videoblog Projects folder and attach your video's screen shot JPEG.

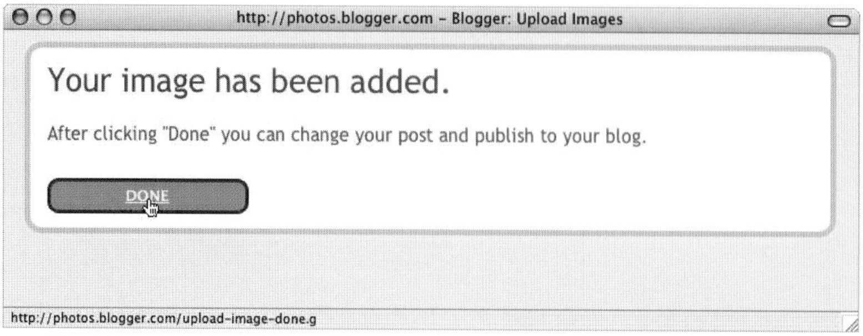

Figure 7.23

Be patient while your photo uploads. When it's done, click the Done button in the pop up window so the image will be placed in your blog post. If you don't click Done, the image will not show up in your post.

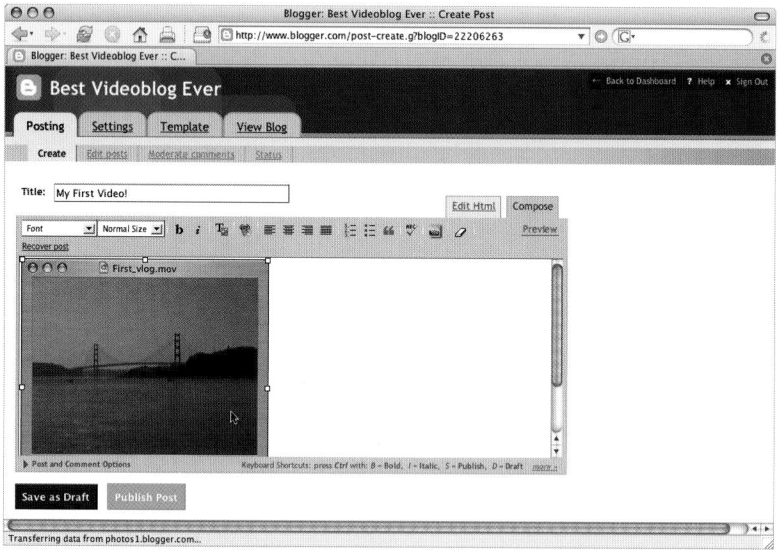

Figure 7.24

Once your image is uploaded, select it by clicking on it. You will know it's selected by the resize box options that appear around it. Click the Link button to link your video URL to the screenshot image.

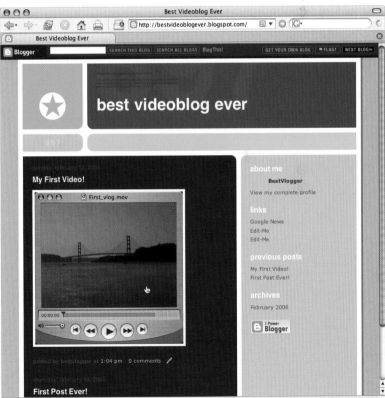

Figure 7.25 Paste your video's URL into the dialog that pops up, then click OK to link the video to your photo. (This will allow your viewers to click on the image and go right to your video.)

Figure 7.26
After you click the orange Publish button on the bottom of the post page and Blogger finishes publishing, click the View Page link to see the finished product.

Combat Comment Spam

Believe it or not, spam plagues vlogs as well as email boxes. The best way to prevent spammers from posting bogus links and advertisements to your comments pages is to turn on a few filters in your Blogger account. In your Blogger Dashboard, click the Change Settings gear icon. In the Settings tab window, click the Comments link up top. You'll see a number of settings. We recommend these:

- For "Who Can Comment?" select Anyone, which allows non-Blogger users to add comments.

- For "Show word verification for comments?" select Yes. Blogger will now ask people to verify a word Blogger shows them in order to post a comment, which demonstrates that they're human and not a spam robot.

- For "Enable comment moderation?" select Yes, and enter your email address in the text field next to "Comment Notification Address." Now any time someone leaves a comment on your blog, Blogger will notify you via email. No comments will be posted publicly without your approval. You will be able to accept or reject a comment before it shows up on your page, which eliminates the possibility that spam will go unnoticed in your comments section.

If you've created a blog and posted your video in the previous steps, you're ready for the next chapter. If you want to explore alternatives to Blogger and Ourmedia, read on.

More Hosting Choices

While Blogger and Ourmedia make it easy to create blogs and post videos, there are other free services. And if you don't mind spending money for a Web hosting service and software, you can even set up your own domain (yet another term for Web address or URL), which lets you choose from a variety of blogging packages and serve up your blog postings and videos in one place.

Free Video Hosting

There are several free video hosting services as well. Blip.tv, at http://blip.tv, is designed specifically for videoblogging and has some special features not available anywhere else (**Figure 7.27**). Not only can you upload and host your video on Blip.tv, but you can also have the service automatically post a video onto your blog and send it to The Archive, which is a big time-saver.

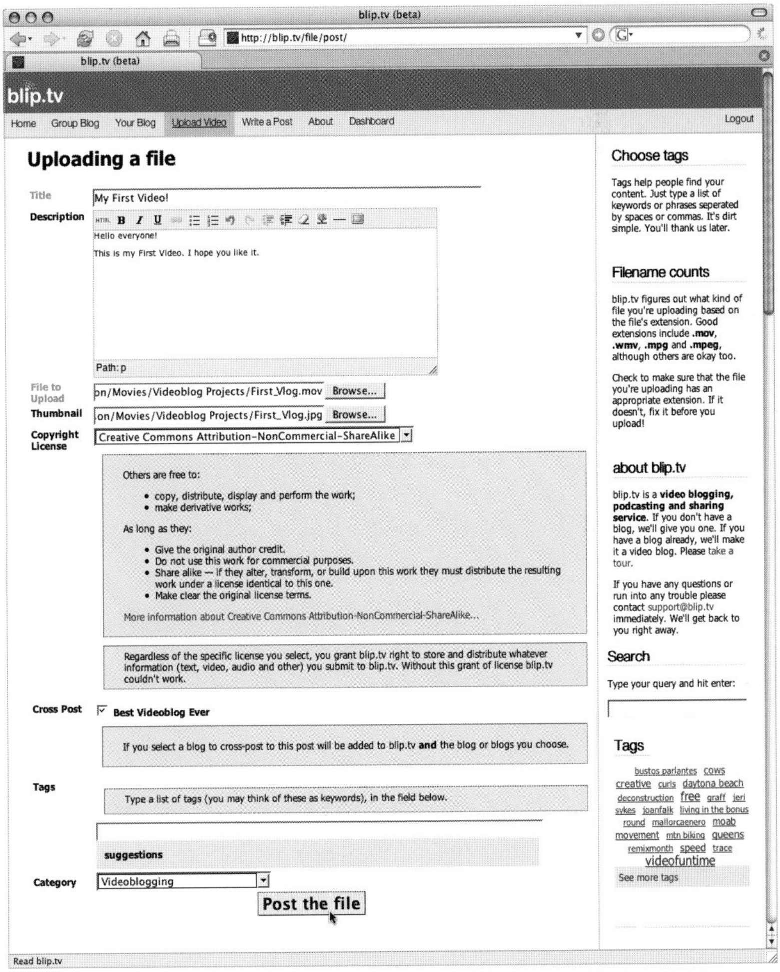

Figure 7.27

The Upload Video page on Blip.tv is set up to act like you're creating a post on your blog, only Blip will host your video and allow you to automatically post it to your blog at the same time. Make sure you add your Blog info into the Share with Others section of your Blip Dashboard and make sure to click the Cross Post button.

Do Not Overlook the Terms Of Use

Many people never bother to read the *terms of use* (also called terms of service) posted on Web sites. But when your creative work is involved, it's a good idea to know what you're agreeing to when you sign up for a hosting service of any kind. Pay particular attention to sections that spell out the rights you are granting to the service. Ourmedia, for example, doesn't require you to assign it any rights. Blip.tv, on the other hand, requires that you give it a non-exclusive license to do anything it wants with your material, as long as it is a noncommercial use

Other services aren't satisfied with having the noncommercial right to your work. Their terms of service use phrases such as "otherwise exploit the User Submissions," "reserves the right to display advertisements in connection with any display of Your Authorized Content," "commercially exploit the User's Videos," and "shall have the right to retain and use any such Information in current or future products or services, without further compensation to you."

You must agree to a site's terms of use when you create an account. Read the terms carefully. If you don't agree with them, find another hosting service. But don't relax entirely. Here's why: Hosting services reserve the right to change their terms of use *at any time* by simply posting the changes online. Don't expect to get a notice if they decide to grab even more rights. So check their terms of service early and often.

Google Video (http://video.google.com), Daily Motion (http://www.dailymotion.com), and YouTube (http://youtube.com), are popular video hosting sites that we can't recommend for videobloggers. One of the reasons is that they distribute your videos in the Flash video format. That's good for viewing on your vlog, but it doesn't work for friends or family who subscribe to vlogs and download videos with a video aggregator like FireAnt.

Taking Control

For the ultimate in blog control and customization, you can register your own Web domain and purchase a Web hosting service to host your Web site for less than $10 per month. This option gives you the greatest control over your videoblog because you can use any blog software you like and serve up lots of videos.

Many videobloggers we know choose Dreamhost (http://dreamhost. com) and 1&1 (http://1and1.com) for Web hosting services and WordPress (http://wordpress.org) and Movable Type (www. sixapart.com/movabletype) software for creating blogs. That doesn't mean establishing your own Web site is easy. Setting up a hosting account and installing blog software can be pretty tricky. Luckily, you can get the flexibility of having your own Web site without the headache of software installation by choosing a hosting provider that does the work for you. Yahoo, for example, supports both WordPress and Movable Type fans. Find WordPress hosting partners at http://wordpress.org/hosting and Movable Type hosting partners at www.sixapart.com/movabletype/hosting.

If even that sounds like too much work, consider an all-in-one service with nothing to install and an easy-to-use Web interface from Six Apart, the company behind Movable Type. The service is called Typepad (http://typepad.com) and it's easier to manage than the do-it-yourself offerings above. Even so, you get video hosting capabilities and customization features for as little as $4.95 per month. If you don't need such features, the free services we've covered in this chapter will do just fine.

Attracting an Audience

So, you've shot your video, edited it, uploaded it, and published it to your vlog. Now it's time to get people to watch it. In this chapter we'll cover how to find and build an audience for your videoblog. You'll learn how to create a videoblog feed, add your vlog to videoblog directories, and announce it to friends, family, and the world. We'll also explain the three benefits of vlog rolls (and how to make one), why and how you should tag your video, and how to collaborate with fellow vloggers.

Setting Up a Subscription Feed

As you may remember from Chapter 1, a vlog feed is the number one key to getting and keeping an audience because it allows viewers to subscribe to a number of videoblogs for automatic updates rather than visiting each one individually. Most blogging services provide feed for their blogs automatically, but they're not always very helpful feeds for videobloggers or vlog subscribers.

For videoblogging, you need an RSS 2.0 feed with enclosures. An enclosure is simply a line of code in the feed that contains a link to the actual video file. That's important because it allows vlog subscribers who use video aggregators like FireAnt and iTunes to automatically download videos from their vlog subscriptions. If your blogging application doesn't provide this kind of feed, we recommend Feedburner, a free service.

So first we'll help you attach the right feed to your vlog so people can subscribe (we'll be using Blogger). Then we'll help you publicize your fabulous new creation.

Creating a Feedburner RSS Feed

The great thing about replacing your default feed with a Feedburner RSS 2.0 feed is that it makes it easy for people to view your video—and all future videos you post. Every time you update your vlog, Feedburner will notify all your subscribers via their aggregators that you've made new content available.

Figure 8.1 Make the switch by opening a browser and going to http://feedburner.com. Enter your videoblog address. Make sure the "I am a podcaster" button to the right of the vlog address field is checked (podcasting and videoblogging use the same type of RSS feeds). This will ensure that a proper RSS 2.0 feed, with media enclosures, is created for your vlog. Click Next.

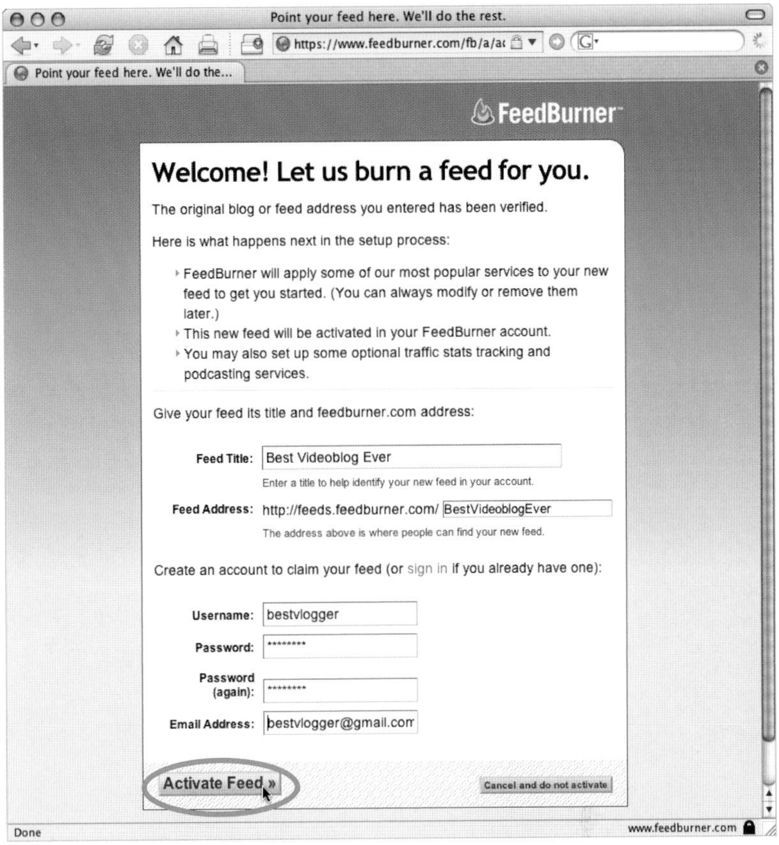

Figure 8.2

Create a Feedburner user name and password. (It's a good idea to use the same user name and password as your vlog so they are easy to remember.) Click Activate Feed.

Figure 8.3

Click the link to Skip
directly to feed
management.

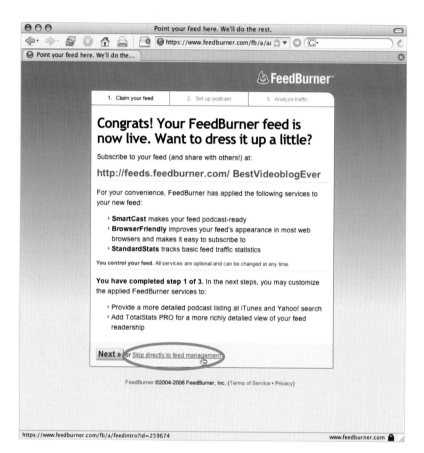

Figure 8.4

In the Feed Management window, click the Publicize tab and from the list of options on the left, click Chicklet Chooser. This will get the HTML code needed to put your feed button on your sidebar.

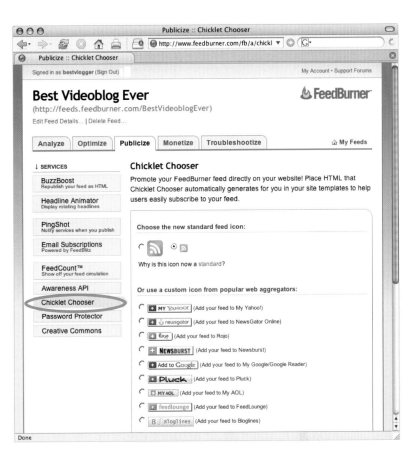

Figure 8.5

Scroll down to select and copy the code in the text field.

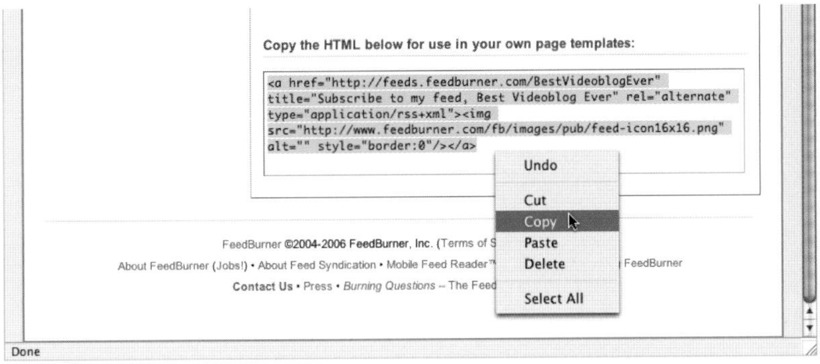

 note   In Firefox, you can press Cmd + T to open your vlog in another tab.

Figure 8.6
Go back to Blogger.com and sign in. In your Blogger Dashboard, click the Change Settings gear icon.

Figure 8.7
Click the Template tab.

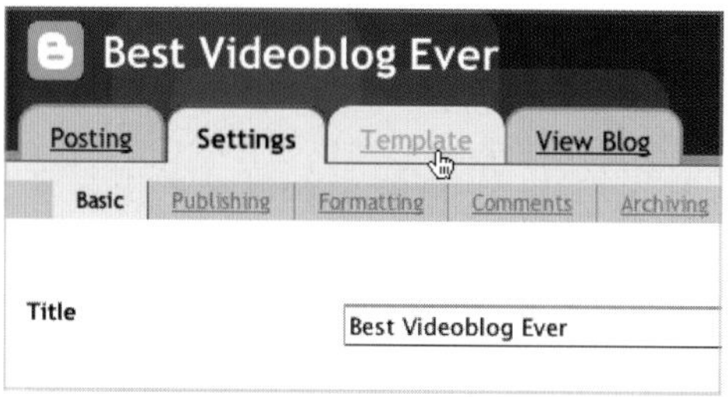

Scroll down almost to the bottom of the Template text field until you see the "I Power Blogger" code that reads:

Figure 8.8 Scroll down almost to the bottom of the Template text field until you see the "I Power Blogger" code that reads:

<p id="powered-by"><a href="http://www.blogger.com"><img src="http://buttons.blogger.com/bloggerbutton1.gif" alt="Powered by Blogger" /></a></p>

Place your cursor immediately above that code and paste in your Feedburner code.

note Sometimes feed buttons don't show up right away. If that happens, click the Refresh button on your browser. Your feed button should show up above the "I Power Blogger" button.

Figure 8.9
Click the Save Template Changes button. At the top of the screen, click the blue Republish button. Finally, after your vlog has republished, click the View Blog link to see the feed button placed on your sidebar.

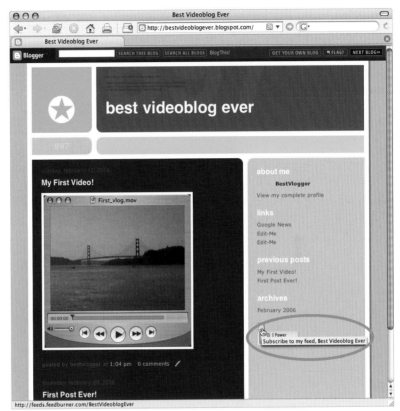

note	If you go to your Blogger Settings tab and click the Site Feed link, you will see that the default Description option is Full. This means the full text of the post will be included in your feed. Don't change this setting. If you do, the enclosures will be removed from your vlog's Feedburner feed.

Publicizing Your Videoblog

You may be vlogging to share moments with people you know, such as your family, friends, or business associates. Or you may want to share your vlog with strangers all across the globe. To get viewers—any viewers—you'll need to announce your videoblog. Here's how to publicize it to videoblog enthusiasts everywhere.

Diving into Directories

In this section we'll show you how to add your videoblog to the FireAnt and Mefeedia directories and then subscribe to it. That way people can begin subscribing to your vlog, and you can test to make sure the RSS feed is working properly.

FireAnt

Figure 8.10 Open up the FireAnt application, and if you use Windows, click the Directory tab.

Figure 8.11

If you use a Mac, click the Directory button and log in. If you don't already have one, create an account at http://fireant.tv.

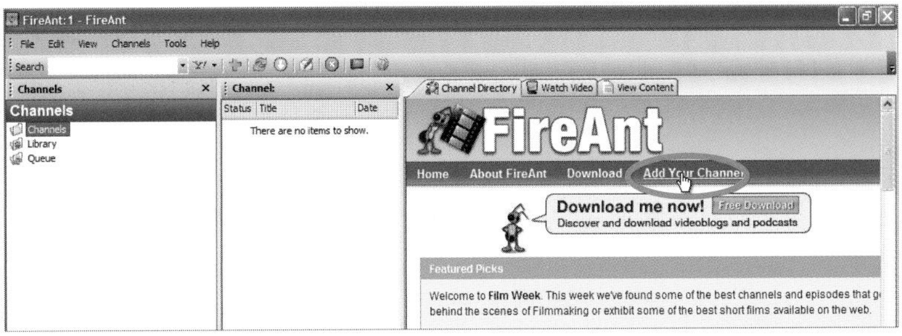

Figure 8.12

Click the Add Your Channel link on the front page of the directory.

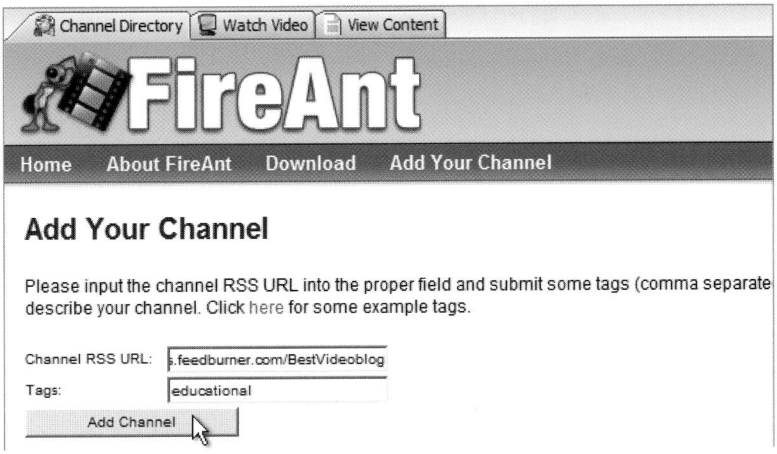

Figure 8.13

Type or paste in the URL for your RSS feed. If you'd like, you can also add a tag or keyword that describes your vlog (see "Tagging Your Videos"). Then click Add Channel.

Figure 8.14

You will get a message saying that your Channel is being held for moderation and will appear in 24 hours. So take a break here. Get some sleep. You deserve it.

note   If lots of new vlogs have been submitted and you miss your vlog's brief appearance on the front page of the FireAnt directory, search for it by name in the directory's search field.

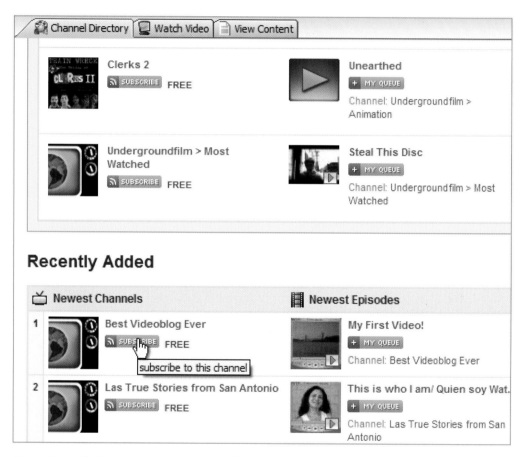

Figure 8.15   If it's been 24 hours since you added your videoblog to FireAnt, you should find it listed on the home page under Recently Added. Now click the Subscribe button to subscribe to your own vlog.

Figure 8.16

If you use Windows, you will see your vlog added under FireAnt's Channels pane with a number indicating how many videos are available.

Figure 8.17

On a Mac, FireAnt shows a dialog giving you a choice of how many items to download for that channel. Choose from all available items, the three most recent items, the most recent item, or nothing. Then click Add Channel.

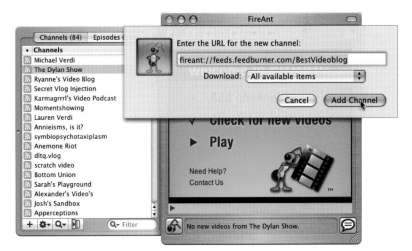

MeFeedia

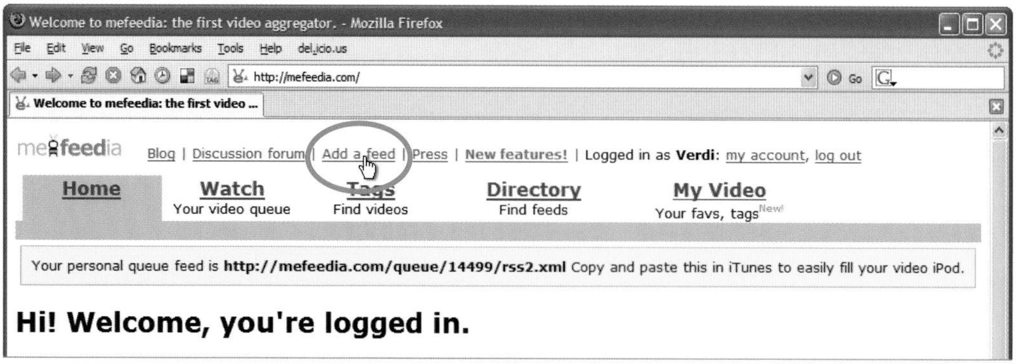

Figure 8.18   Open your browser and go to Mefeedia at http://mefeedia.com. Log in, creating an account first if you haven't already. Then click the Add a feed link at the top of the page.

Figure 8.19

Type or paste in the URL for your RSS feed and then click Add this RSS feed.

Figure 8.20

In a few moments, you will see a message saying it worked. Then click the link to the Feed Details page.

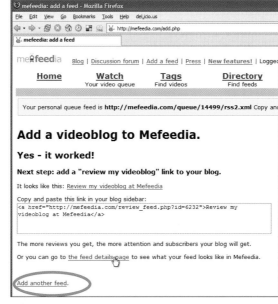

Figure 8.21   The feed details page lists all of your available videos and provides a subscribe button. Click the Subscribe button (which will change to an Unsubscribe button) and a message will appear saying that you are subscribed.

VlogDir, VlogMap, and iTunes

Remember when you used VlogDir, VlogMap, and iTunes to find and view interesting vlogs? Now you can continue your publicizing journey by adding your site to these directories as well (**Figures 8.22** to **8.24**).

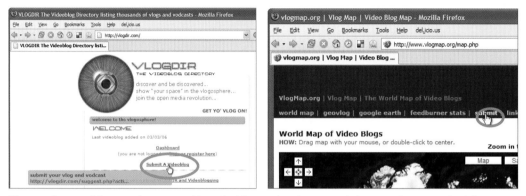

Figures 8.22 and 8.23   It's easy to add a videoblog to the VlogDir and VlogMap directories by following the Submit links on their home pages.

Figure 8.24
To add a vlog to iTunes, follow the Submit a Podcast link on the front page of the Podcast section of the Music Store.

note   To submit your feed to the iTunes directory, you need an iTunes Music Store account. Getting an account requires a credit card or PayPal account, which won't be charged unless you download music.

Tagging Your Videos

Another way to publicize your vlog is through the use of tags. A tag is a label or keyword such as *music, knitting,* or *San Francisco* that describes a video, and videos can have more than one tag. Tags help people find your video more easily when they search video directories. You can add tags for searches on Ourmedia and Blip.tv during the upload process. You can also tag your videos within Mefeedia on your video queue page or in FireAnt through its directory.

One nice thing about tags is that each one can have an RSS feed associated with it, so people can subscribe to a tag (or topic) itself. Earlier you subscribed to your vlog in Mefeedia and FireAnt. Now you can use those directories to tag your video.

Figure 8.25

Sign in to Mefeedia, go to your video queue and play one of your videos. Then simply click the Tag This button under the video and enter a descriptive word for your video. Then click Tag.

Figure 8.26

To view the videos that you've tagged, click the Tags link at the top of the page.

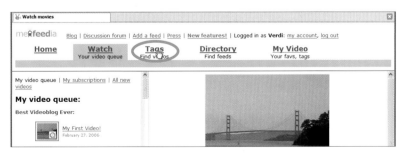

Figure 8.27   On the Tags page, click See my personal tags.

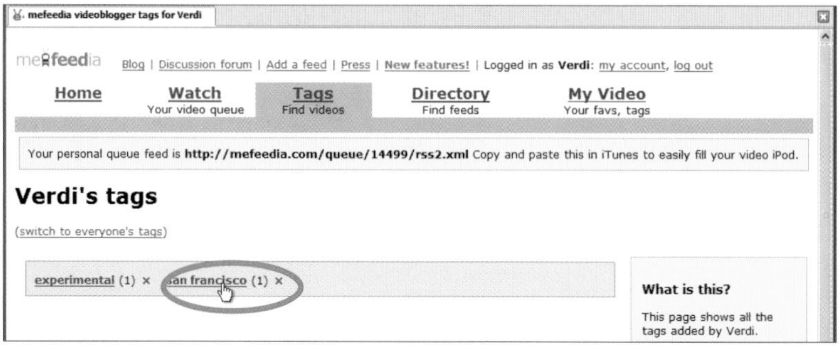

Figure 8.28   Click on one of the listed tags to see the videos that have that tag attached to it. The page changes to show all the videos you've marked with a particular tag—in this case "San Francisco." Anytime you tag another video with this same tag, it will automatically be added to this page.

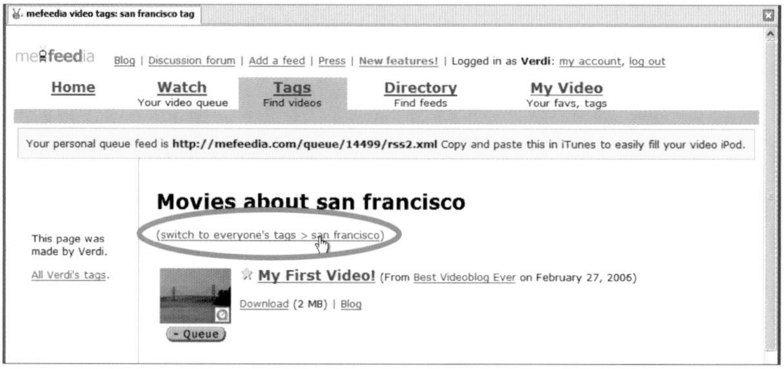

Figure 8.29   To see all the videos that Mefeedia users have tagged "San Francisco," click Switch to everyone's tags.

Figure 8.30

The RSS 2.0 feed button at the bottom of this page will let anyone subscribe to this tag. Click it if you want to subscribe to the tag you attached to your video.

Telling People You Know

How do you introduce friends and family to your videoblog? Your best bet is to simply email a URL to everyone you want to see it (see "Link Savvy"). You can do that in a couple of ways that are probably already familiar. The simplest is just to copy your vlog's URL from the browser and paste it into the body of your email. Don't forget to tell viewers how to subscribe to your videoblog through an aggregator, as we explained in Chapter 1.

Link Savvy

Usually you'll want to give out the general Web address for your videoblog, but not always. When you thank friends for participating in a shoot, for example, you'll want to point to the specific video they helped create. That's easy to do because most blog services automatically create a unique page with a unique URL for each post and the comments about that post. This permanent link, or *permalink*, to the unique page for each post can be difficult to find if you don't know what it looks like.

In Blogger sites, as in many others, the permalink is located at the bottom of each post as a timestamp. Click the permalink as shown here to go to the permanent page for that posting, read all the comments about it, or to copy its unique URL. Click the comments link to the right to go to the comments form and respond to comments.

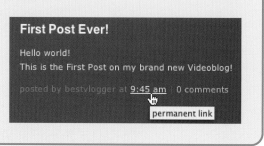

Depending on the type of vlog you create, you may want to tell clients and business associates about it. Diana, for example, uses her vlog at http://weynand.blogspot.com/2006/02/los-angeles-class.html to reach training clients old and new **(Figure 8.31)**. You can also spread the news effectively by adding the URL to the email signature file that's automatically added to the end of your messages. (If you're not sure how, check the Help section of your email program.) Just a link and a short note asking people to check out your new videoblog will do the trick.

Figure 8.31
Business vlogs are still relatively rare. Diana uses her Weynand Training vlog to connect with students.

Interacting with Your Audience

The blog part of your videoblog was designed for interaction. That's where you write about each video you create and add related info and links. Subscribers automatically receive each post with a link to your video, and they and other viewers can comment on your work. You, in turn, can choose whether or not you want to respond to those comments. How much or how little you interact with your audience—and fellow vloggers—is up to you.

Some people are happy to collect a few "nice work" comments and leave it at that. Other vloggers pay careful attention to the comments they receive and follow the Web links left by visitors to discover more about them. Many interesting collaborations, including the one that gave rise to this book, were born of connections discovered in the comments section of a vlog.

Spreading the Word

One way to announce your vlog to a mass audience is to join the video-blogging e-mail list at http://groups.yahoo.com/group/videoblogging. This list was started with only about five videobloggers and has grown over the past two years to more than 2,000 participants. Letting these hardcore videoblog enthusiasts know that you exist is a great way to start becoming a part of that community. So send an introduction with your vlog address and the URL of your feed.

Part of the fun of vlogging is connecting with people who have similar interests. Post your vlog address to forums and message boards for people who may share similar passions. Is your videoblog about knitting? Announce your vlog on knitting sites to get enthusiasts excited about your videoblog. You might even encourage others to make videoblogs for trading hobby tips, tricks, and secrets.

Creating a Vlog Roll

In Chapter 1, we encouraged you to explore videoblogs through links on vloggers' sidebars or vlog rolls (see "Vlog Rolls and Directories"). A vlog roll is a kind of triple threat. First, it lets you interact with your audience by recommending other videoblogs. Then too, in recommending other videoblogs, you're actively participating in the community. Finally, a vlog roll promotes your videoblog to the vloggers on your vlog roll. They don't have to link back to your videoblog, but they might.

Creating a vlog roll is certainly not required for a novice vlogger, but it's not difficult to do. (If you don't want to do it now, you can always come back to it when you're ready to customize your vlog.) Adding links to your vlog's sidebar is pretty simple once you know where to look for the key HTML information in your Template. Keep reading and we'll show you in Blogger.

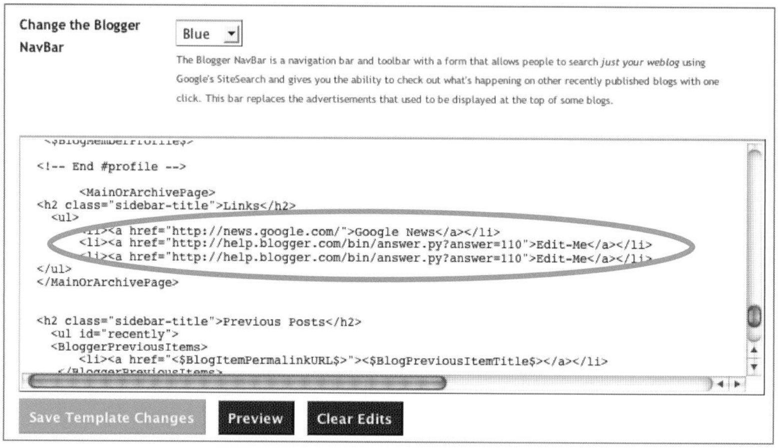

Figure 8.32
In your Blogger Dashboard, click the Template tab. In the HTML text box, scroll down toward the bottom of your template code to the Links section that contains the Google News, Edit Me and Edit Me links.

Change the words "Edit Me" to the *name* of the vlog you want to link to. Change the *link address* to the URL of the vlog you are linking to.

If you were linking to www.momentshowing.net, for example, your code to create a text link would look like this:

    <a href="http://www.momentshowing.net>Momentshowing</a>

To add a graphic or a button instead of text, add a piece of code for the image source, the location of the graphic on the Web, where the "Edit Me" text is. (You can grab the image source of a graphic by right clicking or control clicking and selecting Copy Link Location.)

If you wanted to add a link to VlogMap, for example, it would look like the line below.

    <a href=http://vlogmap.org><img src=www.server.com/image.jpg></a>

Figure 8.33
At the bottom of the Template tab, click Save Template Changes, and then click Republish.

Figure 8.34
Once you have republished the changes, click View blog. Your sidebar will now have the text link and the button link.

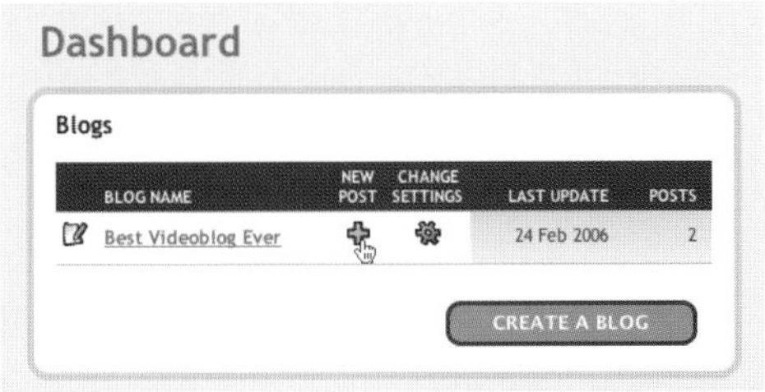

Figure 8.35
If you want to upload your own graphic for use on your sidebar, you can use the Blogger server as if you were uploading a JPEG for a video post. Go to your Blogger Dashboard and create a new post on your blog.

Figure 8.36
Click the Add Image button, find the image on your computer, and upload it to your blog post.

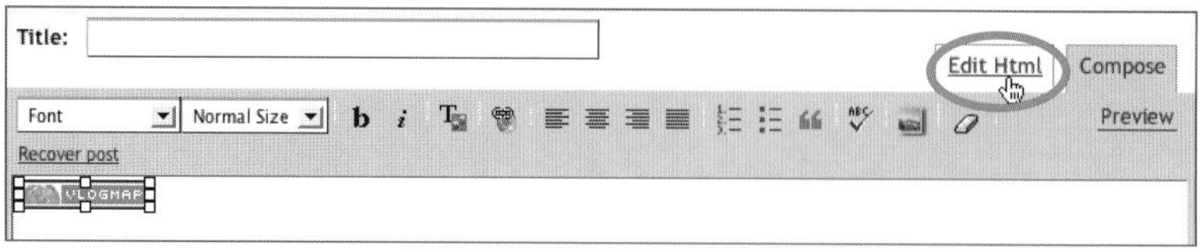

Figure 8.37

Your image will show up in your post window, but you need to grab the image source address of where it lives on Blogger's servers. Click the Edit HTML tab in your post window.

Figure 8.38

Select the first photo URL location and copy the image address code.

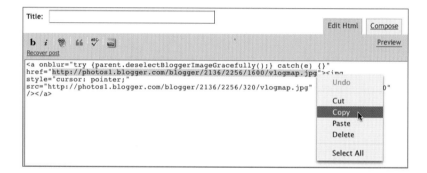

Click the Template tab and paste this image address into your links section using the code below and as shown in **Figure 8.39**.

<a href=http://vlogmap.org><img src=www.server.com/image.jpg></a>

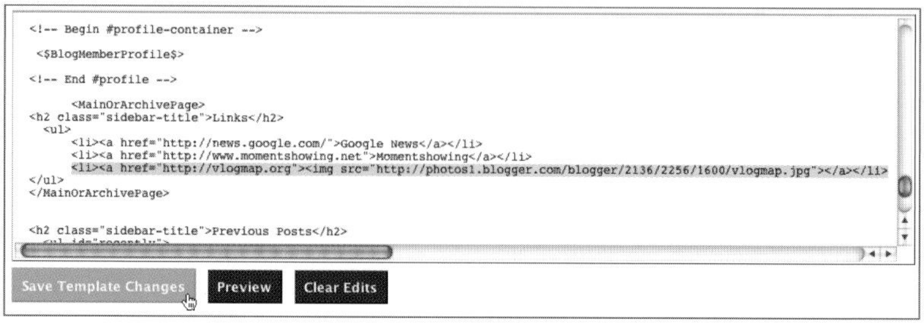

Figure 8.39

Click Save Template Changes and then Republish. Click View Blog to see the image on your sidebar.

Collaborating with Vloggers

When you vlog, you're sure to make some videoblogger friends. How do you collaborate with them if they live on the other side of the world? The answer, of course, is the Internet. Instead of collaborating side by side, some videobloggers are using special sections of their videoblogs to collaborate with other vloggers; others make completely new videoblogs to collect work for special group projects.

Bottom Union, for example, created a short promotional video for a fictional product called Carp Caviar and then invited others to participate by creating their own versions. Over the next two months, 50 Carp Caviar promos were collected from videobloggers all over the world (**Figure 8.40**).

Figure 8.40

Bottom Union's Carp Caviar project, lives on as a weekly collaboration at http://bottomunion .com/blog/?cat=16.

To celebrate the one-year anniversary of Lo-Fi Saint Louis, Bill Streeter decided to rerun a month of his favorite videos, with introductions by 28 different videobloggers (**Figure 8.41**).

Figure 8.41

Bill Streeter of Lo-Fi Saint Louis asked fellow vloggers to help him celebrate the vlog's first birthday. View the results at http://lofistl.com/?cat=45.

Videobloggers Raymond M. Kristiansen, from Norway, and Michael Meiser, from Chicago, started Evilutionary Virtual Log, or Evilvlog, as a group effort. The vlog, at http://evilvlog.com, has about 30 contributors (**Figure 8.42**).

Figure 8.42
Evilvlog, the Evilutionary Virtual Log, is like a digital sandbox where people experiment and try things out.

Sample, Remix, and Mashup

Using one of the Creative Commons licenses that allow derivative works (See "Creative Commons" in Chapter 2), vloggers have the ability to take a piece of someone else's video and create something new with it. In the music world, this practice is commonly referred to as *sampling*, *remixing*, or a *mashup*, and those terms are becoming common among videobloggers too. The Squeeze project was started when Charlene of Scratch Video remixed a video posted on Mica's videoblog, Hello? Others joined in and continued to remix the remixes (**Figure 8.43**).

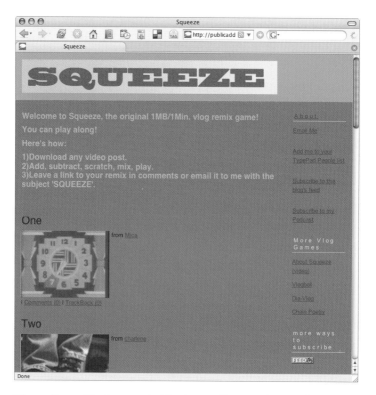

Figure 8.43   The Squeeze Archive has a collection of remixed videos at http://publicaddress.typepad.com/squeeze. You can play the vlog-remix game by following the steps on the Web site.

Remixing and mashups are so much fun that the vlog news site We Are The Media, at http://wearethemedia.com, ran a month-long contest appropriately named Remixoff (**Figure 8.44**).

Figure 8.44

Dozens of videobloggers participated in the Remixoff competition. View the winners at http://wearethemedia.com/2005/12/14/remix-champions.

For the Remixoff contest, contestants published videos on their vlogs and then they "tagged" the videos *remixoff2005* (see "Collaborating with Tags"). The people behind We Are The Media were able to collect all the entries simply by searching for the remixoff2005 tag.

Collaborating with Tags

Chosen carefully, tags can act like folders in a filing cabinet. Just as a folder can contain many related documents, a tag can connect many related videos for a specific project. If you assign a unique tag to a group project, it becomes easy for people to track all of the videos created for the project. Last year, for example, Michael made a seminal video about the meaning of videoblogging called "Vlog Anarchy."

"I've been wanting to get this off my chest for a long time," he wrote in the post. "Don't leave me any text comments—make a video instead and post the link. Also, go to Mefeedia and tag your video 'vlog anarchy' and I'll post the RSS feed." You can see the results of this passionate conversation at http://mefeedia.com/tags/vloganarchy.

Expanding the Community

Announcing and sharing your videoblog with family, friends, and associates may require a little education. Techie friends won't require much explanation as to how and why it all works. But others may need you to take some time and really show them what vlogging is all about. Remember our mantra when explaining the all-encompassing coolness of videoblogs: They're like Web sites but easily updatable, archive-able, and subscribe-able. Like the Web, the videoblogging community becomes more interesting, and more useful, as more people join it.

So if you find that you enjoy educating people about videoblogs and want to help them start their own, please check out our NODE101 project at http://node101.org. NODE101 was founded by four videobloggers—Michael, Ryanne, Jay Dedman, and Josh Kinberg—to create local media centers where people can teach each other to videoblog, collaborate, and simply hang out. If there isn't a NODE where you live, consider starting one.

Epilogue

Because videoblogging shares a lot of the visual language of television and film, people often consider it just a new twist on old, established media. But videoblogging is profoundly different from its relatives. First of all, unlike conventional television and film, it's a medium that is open to anyone with a few relatively simple, affordable tools. More significantly, though, instead of being a one-way communication from creator to consumer, like traditional media (not just movies and TV, but newspapers and magazines as well), vlogging is about creating conversations among members of a global community.

Vloggers give us a fresh look at the world—a vlogosphere that's not limited by geography, where people create communities. We may not all speak the same language, but post a vlog to the Internet showing your grandmother, the town that you live in, or whatever your passion may be, and you can communicate with anyone anywhere.

We had a simple motivation for writing this book: We wanted to encourage more people to join in the conversation. The more people participate—by subscribing to vlogs, viewing and commenting on them, and posting their own—the more compelling and meaningful the conversation becomes.

So now that you've harnessed this amazing new communication tool, please help us spread the word. Tell people about your own videoblog, share your favorite vlogs with them, and explain how to subscribe to vlogs.

And tell us what you're vlogging about so we can help promote you. Ryanne and Michael list new videoblogs on Freevlog

(http://freevlog.org/wordpress/index.php/category/new-vlogs).
Write to us at newvlog@freevlog.org with your vlog's address and
the feed URL so you can be included.

Although we've come to the end of this book, vlogging has barely
begun. If you're wondering what's next, believe us, we are too. How
the vlogosphere grows and evolves is up to us all. We're sure of only
one thing: wherever it leads will be truly astounding.

Index